TOTAL QUALITY CONTROL FOR MANAGEMENT

STRATEGIES AND TECHNIQUES FROM TOYOTA AND TOYODA GOSEI

Total Quality Control for Management

Strategies and Techniques from Toyota and Toyoda Gosei

by

Masao Nemoto

Translated and Edited by David Lu

Originally Titled: TQC TO TOPPU BUKACHOU
NO YAKUWARI (Total Quality Control for
Management)

PRENTICE HALL, INC.   **Englewood Cliffs, N.J.**

Prentice-Hall International, Inc., *London*
Prentice-Hall of Australia, Pty. Ltd., *Sydney*
Prentice-Hall Canada, Inc., *Toronto*
Prentice-Hall of India Private Ltd., *New Delhi*
Prentice-Hall of Japan, Inc., *Tokyo*
Prentice-Hall of Southeast Asia Pte. Ltd., *Singapore*
Editora Prentice-Hall do Brasil Ltda., *Rio de Janeiro*
Prentice-Hall Hispanoamericana, S.A., *Mexico*

Originally printed in Japan
as *TQC TO TOPPU BU-
KACHOU NO YAKU-
WARI (Total Quality
Control for Management)*
by Masao Nemoto. © 1983
and 1986 by Masao Nem-
oto. English translation
rights arranged with JUSE
Press, Ltd. through Japan
Foreign-Rights Centre.

10 9 8 7 6 5 4 3 2

Library of Congress Cataloging-in-Publication Data

Nemoto, Masao.
    Total quality control for management.

    Translation of: TQC to Toppu Bukachou no yakuwari.
    Includes index.
    1. Quality circles. 2. Quality control. I. Lu,
David J. (David John) II. Title.
HD66.N4613 1987   658.4′036   87-2329

ISBN 0-13-925637-7

Printed in the United States of America

Introduction
to the Original
Japanese Edition

Mr. Masao Nemoto, President of Toyoda Gosei, has decided to publish a book on total quality control (TQC). Mr. Nemoto was a managing director of Toyota Motors in charge of production engineering and quality assurance before he took up his present position in the fall of 1982. During his tenure at Toyota Motors, Mr. Nemoto was the central figure in its TQC promotion.

Toyota Motors has had more than two decades of experience in TQC, and Mr. Nemoto has left us with many significant and lasting contributions. Among them was the QC education for Toyota affiliates which he initiated when he was division manager of purchasing control. It was the first of its kind in Japan, and was exceptionally well-received by all who were connected with it and by the general public. Today, we can point with pride to the high levels of attainment reached by our affiliated plants. I am confident that this is due in no small measure to the expert guidance they received from Mr. Nemoto.

Mr. Nemoto is also a manager with rich experience in annual policy control. From the time he was a division manager to the time he became one of our managing directors, for a period of close to 20 years, Mr. Nemoto selected his own annual policies, and taught his subordinates in the fine art of policy control through their implementation. He is one of the very few practitioners of this art who can also claim more than 20 years of experience.

Not long ago, many Toyota dealers expressed an interest in introducing QC-type management to their dealerships. Mr. Nemoto, who was then one of our managing directors, was the logical choice to help promote this worthy program. For a period of two years, he donated his Saturdays and Sundays and visited more than 300 dealerships across the country. His lectures and expert guidance helped persuade 90 percent of Toyota dealers to introduce QC. I am grateful to Mr. Nemoto for his tireless efforts and persuasive presentations.

As president of Toyoda Gosei, Mr. Nemoto is showing his mastery of the art of management. He has initiated several epoch-making changes in Toyoda Gosei which are worthy of observation and respect by many of us. I look forward to seeing more of his many-splendored accomplishments unfold.

Indeed Mr. Nemoto is a great administrator, manager and educator. This book, based on his many years of rich experience, is an unusual compendium of TQC implementation and know-how. It is edited to suit the needs of business people. I highly recommend this book not only to those of you who are in manufacturing but also to others in service industries.

Shoichiro Toyoda
President, Toyota Motors
August 1983

Author's Preface to the First Book

During the past two years, I spoke three times at the National Meeting of Quality Control and Standardization. My three speeches were generally based on my own experiences as a manager and administrator. I was encouraged and profoundly grateful in receiving so many comments and questions. There were also requests from various companies to come to speak, but time did not really permit it.

As I was feeling uncomfortable saying "No" to many kind invitations, a suggestion came from Mrs. Haruko Mitsuaki of the JUSE press that I rewrite my speeches in book form. She indicated that there were many requests coming to her for tapes of my speeches. My seniors in the Toyota group, including the chairman, president and senior advisors, were all very encouraging. They wanted me to write a book which would be useful to other managers and administrators.

It has been more than 30 years since I first became a manager. During these three decades, I have received numerous suggestions and instructions from many people. I also have a few experiences, improvements, and credos of my own to add. I decided to write this book (Part I in the English translation) as a small token of my appreciation to those people who have been good to me, including teachers, senior officers of the company, colleagues and subordinates who have played a part in nurturing my growth.

In this book, I have included a large number of questions and answers. I hope that most of the questions addressed to me at one time or another are adequately answered. If there are still questions remaining, I hope to add them when a revised edition becomes available.

I wish to take this opportunity to thank my teachers and seniors for their unfailing help and support. I only wish I could visit each and every one of them individually to offer my gratitude. Thanks are also due to the editorial staff of the JUSE press, and to Mr. Okochi, a division manager at Toyoda Gosei, for their help, efforts and kindness.

Masao Nemoto
September 1983

Author's Preface
to the Second Book

My previous book (Part I in the English translation), which was published in September 1983, was read by more than 70,000 people within two and a half years of its publication. It received the Nikkei Quality Control Literature Prize in 1984, and has been translated into French. In 1987, we expect that an English edition will appear in the United States.

The other day, Professor David Lu of Bucknell University from the United States came to see me. In translating my work into English, he wanted to add some information about my past two years' TQC activities, and suggested that I write about them for the American audience. After consulting with Mrs. Haruko Mitsuaki of the JUSE press, I decided to bring out this new edition.

This volume (Part II in the English translation) centers around the events of the past three years, from the time I left Toyota Motors to become president of Toyoda Gosei. The strengthening of Toyoda Gosei's special corporate attributes (*taishitsu*) through the practice of TQC led to being awarded the Deming application prize in 1985. This book relates the events leading to the receipt of that prize, chronicling the sweat and tears we experienced as part of the narrative.

Within five years, we plan to meet the challenge of the Japan Quality Medal, awarded only to a select few companies which have been previously awarded the Deming application prize. In Chapter 4 (Chapter 10 in the English translation), I am presenting the concept of our groupwide TQC, which I plan to use as one of the activities to be examined for the Medal.

Chapter 5 (Chapter 11 in the English translation) contains my suggestions for diversifying QC circle activities. I would welcome your reactions to them.

The previous volume (Part I) referred frequently to my own experiences, sometimes giving the appearance of a book of excerpts from the records of my activities. In the present volume (Part II), I have attempted to make my discussion more comprehensive and universal. It is my hope that the present volume can be helpful not only to my new readers but also to my old friends who have read the previous book.

Masao Nemoto
April 1986

AUTHOR'S NOTES FOR THE ENGLISH EDITION

I have asked Professor Lu to combine the two books into one for the English edition, and edit out some of the materials which may overlap in the two books. For the readers who are not familiar with quality control, may I suggest that this book be read alongside Professor Kaoru Ishikawa's standard work, *What Is Total Quality Control? The Japanese Way.*

There is no greater joy for me than to see that my American friends find this book useful. To me it is something in the nature of repaying the kindness which you have so generously shown to us.

Masao Nemoto

Translator's Introduction

Stepping one day into the Haruhi plant of Toyoda Gosei in the fall of 1985, I was struck by the lack of unpleasant odors which often characterize factories which manufacture rubber products. The plant was kept meticulously clean.

The second sight was even more noteworthy. I was accompanying Mr. Nemoto, the author of this book, on one of his rounds through the plant. There, an unusual event was unfolding before my very eyes. Workers without hesitation stopped their president and asked if he could spend a few minutes with them. Some of the conversations were casual, but some were in the nature of serious reports for which decisions would have to be made. Mr. Nemoto would nod, say a few words, consult with the Assistant Plant Manager, who was also with us, and render his decision. There was very little time wasted, and the workers looked content. I was witnessing a master at work in his own speciality—that of managing a company, and doing it well.

I consider Mr. Nemoto to be one of the very best managers that present-day Japan has produced. When we speak of the effectiveness of Japan's management techniques, we often refer to the Toyota production system, which, with the working of its KANBAN and Just-in-Time systems, has enabled Toyota to produce world-class cars at a competitive cost. The other pillar of Japan's management system is in its application of quality control. Japanese products sell well overseas simply because they try to make them better. And to attain this reputation, quality control has been in the forefront of its efforts.

While the twin pillars of Japanese management techniques are widely practiced, we seldom see the two systems converge to make a unified system viable in its own right. This is where Mr. Nemoto comes in. His management style is that of combining these twin pillars, and he has a unique background which has made this possible.

Masao Nemoto was born in Kagoshima prefecture in the southern island of Kyushu. Immediately after his graduation from the Tokyo Institute of Technology in 1943, he entered Toyota Motors, but was assigned to naval duty as a technical officer. After the war he resumed his work at Toyota where he saw the virtue of job rotation firsthand. The assignments he received included: safety, assembly, painting, production control and machining. In 1966 he was appointed division manager of purchasing control. In 1970, he was a company director. He concurrently served as plant manager at the Motomachi and Miyoshi plants at one time, and the Tsutsumi and Myochi plants at another time. In 1976, he was appointed a managing director. In that capacity, he oversaw a number of divisions, including the divisions of purchasing, production engineering and quality assurance and computer. The experiences he acquired at Toyota were many and varied. They included areas of proper engineering techniques and management techniques. He felt that Mr. Eiji Toyoda, presently the chairman of Toyota Motors, wanted him to have as wide an amount of experience as possible so he might become a man who could break down the walls of sectionalism in Toyota.

It is also in this ability to break down the walls of sectionalism that Mr. Nemoto has distinguished himself as president of Toyoda Gosei, the position he has held since the fall of 1982. Under him, interdivisional communication has become much better. He has also extended that principle in his dealings with his subordinates. His management style is one of respect for humanity. People may work for him, but their worth as individuals is fully appreciated by him. He does not scold, and creates an atmosphere which is easy for everyone to speak his mind. I remember when his chauffeur took me to Nagoya station, a ride of about 45 minutes from Toyoda Gosei. When asked about his dealings with Mr. Nemoto, he did not hesitate to volunteer the information that he has never been scolded by him. Simple as it may appear, this approach has earned him adulation, respect and love from his subordinates.

Then there is his relationship with his subcontractors, referred to in this book as Toyoda Gosei affiliates. Again the walls of separation are disappearing, which helps both Toyoda Gosei and the affiliates to produce quality products more efficiently and with less lead time. The strength of Japan's major industries may well be found in their ability to maintain closer relations with their suppliers. Here Mr. Nemoto shows us how this system really works.

Unlike other books on quality control, Mr. Nemoto's is characterized by its homespun wisdom. If others tend to be too theoretical, Nemoto's leans heavily toward practicality. But the implication goes beyond this. Some practitioners of QC in Japan argue that QC equals management, and it represents everything that need be known in management. This view has alienated some Japanese managers from QC, and is certainly not the one with which Mr. Nemoto identifies himself. With his rich experience behind him, Mr. Nemoto delimits the utility of QC. By defining QC in this particular manner, he has made it far more approachable to thousands of other managers. In fact, if you have any doubt about the advisability of having QC in your company, you may wish to use the Nemoto approach as outlined in this volume.

The present edition is a translation of two books by Mr. Nemoto, the first one which was published in 1983, and its sequel which was published in 1986. In this edition they are represented as Part I and Part II. Some people who read this volume along with the Japanese original or French translation may find slight discrepancies in the materials contained. This is caused by several factors:

1. Mr. Nemoto expressly rewrote a number of paragraphs for his American audience which are fully translated in this book.

2. At the end of Part I, the Japanese original contains a section of illustrated materials showing abnormality control and other activities at Toyoda Gosei. These illustrations are mainly for use by the foremen on the floor. Thus they are not included in the English edition. The substance of these materials are, however, fully described in the text.

3. Materials which are duplicated in both parts, and some specific questions dealing with the workings of the Deming prize, which are of interest primarily to those Japanese executives who are also interested in applying for the prize, are also omitted from this translation.

As you read through this book, you will be impressed by the warmth of Mr. Nemoto's personality. It has been a factor in creating a *lively workplace* everywhere he has been. And in this volume, you will find two instances in which Mrs. Nemoto also becomes a practitioner of QC at home. There is a charming, infectious quality to the happy practice of QC. Mrs. Nemoto may be interested to note that my wife too has been speaking in QC terms as she has read through this translation!

It has been a pleasure knowing Mr. Nemoto personally and through this book. I wish to take this opportunity to thank him for his unfailing courtesy. Thanks are also due to Mrs. Haruko Mitsuaki of the JUSE press and Mrs. Bette Schwartzberg of Prentice-Hall, two ladies who have never met, but are united in the common goal of disseminating vital knowledge across the Pacific for the benefit of both of our countries.

David J. Lu

Table of Contents

Part I

Strengthening Corporate Attributes and Motivating Employees

Chapter 1. Improvement After Improvement—My Credo . 3

Improvement after improvement; Good coordination with other divisions; Everyone speaks; Reason for not scolding; Try harder when you teach, if the other party does not understand; Send out your best subordinates for rotation; A command without a deadline is not a command; Rehearsal is an ideal occasion for training; Inspection itself is a failure if there is no top involvement; Opportunity to be heard by the top.

Chapter 2. Efficiency in Administrative Divisions and Technology-Related Divisions **21**

Why did we decide to promote efficiency?; Efficiency target; Methods of promoting the efficiency movement; Conditions at our take-off stage; Interim inspection of March 1983; Problems remaining and how to proceed in the future; Questions and answers.

Table of Contents

Table of Contents

I

STRENGTHENING CORPORATE ATTRIBUTES AND MOTIVATING EMPLOYEES

1

Improvement
After Improvement—
My Credo

Whenever I am transferred to a new post, I give an itemized document to my new associates explaining my views on management and on the manner in which work must be conducted. On matters that I need to emphasize, I often use slogan-like expressions to drive home what I want to say.

Some of my associates have compiled these words of mine into the "Sayings of Nemoto." In this chapter, I am reproducing and adding some explanations to 10 items from these "sayings." Many of the thoughts expressed in this chapter are not necessarily new. They owe a great deal to those people who have trodden the same path before me and to many specialists in the field. I may simply express similar views with different words. But in any event, these 10 items represent my considered judgment fortified by many years of practice. Through practice, confidence is gained—and in some areas improvements are made.

As you read this chapter, please do not probe each of the items for its imperfection, but take the 10 items as a whole to get an overall view of my ideas.

I. Improvement After Improvement

"What is your credo?" When reporters come to interview me, they often begin with this question. My response has always been: "Improvement after improvement." It has been my guiding principle in my more than three decades of service with Toyota Motors and its affiliates.

During the first 10 years, I was involved mainly with manufacturing, and my activities centered around work improvement and improvement of office procedures. These included matters such as: how to improve the way we handle our work, minor improvement of facilities and equipment, improvement in recordkeeping procedures and improvement in instructional methods. I endeavored to create an atmosphere which was conducive to raising our ability for improvement. An instructor's license I held in the "training within industry (TWI)" was a definite plus. While utilizing my own ideas, I never forgot to solicit ideas actively from those supervisors who worked for me.

This decade coincided with the period when Toyota was thoroughly training its employees in the now well-known Toyota production system. As a TWI instructor, I worked day and night to inculcate the virtue of the Toyota system to the employees who worked under me. It was a period filled with "improvement after improvement."

The next two decades comprised a period when quality control (QC) became a major concern. We began the study of quality control on a companywide basis in 1963.

QC gave us a means to challenge the status quo, and the so-called control circle of "plan, do, check, action" did serve our needs well. It was an exhilarating experience to be exposed to the idea of establishing an annual policy to which I previously had paid scant attention. I was determined to master its techniques, and thereafter paid special attention to the control of annual policy. There were many improvement projects which had to be completed within six months or a year. I was impressed with the structure of the annual policy which always allowed incorporation of these projects with a view to their implementation.

In 1965, Toyota Motors received the Deming application prize which was followed by the award in 1970 of the Japan Quality Control Medal. My own involvement included providing instruction in total quality control (TQC) for affiliated plants, improving purchasing activities from the standpoint of quality control, improving quality, quantity and cost at various plants as their plant manager, promoting QC circle activities, improving manufacturing technology and quality assurance, enhancing managerial abilities of top and middle management, promoting QC activities with dealers across the country and establishing greater efficiency in office procedures. I have been immersed in "improvement after improvement" with QC always at my side. My life has been guided by the continuum of "improvement after improvement," and I know this will remain my guiding principle.

II. Good Coordination with Other Divisions Is an Essential Quality for Middle Managers

As a company becomes larger and more divisions are created, it becomes an important concern for the company to be able to coordinate smoothly the work which overlaps several divisions. While it is the responsibility of top management to solve problems related to this, that responsibility must be shared by middle management who assists the top.

My advice to division managers has been as follows: "It is not enough to manage the affairs within your own division. One of the most important functions of a division manager is to improve coordination between his own division and other divisions. If you cannot handle this task, please go to work for an American company." As I understand it, in the United States, the functions of a division manager are clearly defined in his job description, and he is hired for these specific functions. Thus it is not conceivable for one division manager to perform the task assigned to another division. However, even in America, things seem to be changing these days.

Japanese companies are in the process of rapid transition. At each division, the tasks assigned to it are constantly changed and improved. This means that improvement is also required in interdivisional coordination. In most companies where I have had either managerial or instructional responsibilities the past several years, the rule of thumb has been that no important task is to be assigned exclusively to one division. Important tasks almost always overlap. In assessing the capabilities of a middle manager, his ability to coordinate interdivisional issues thus becomes a key factor.

Now as to the means of strengthening the ability of these middle managers, I continue to emphasize the following three points.

The first point is to let all the division managers know that top management considers coordination between divisions very important. Why not emphasize this point by saying to your division managers that "Anyone who cannot coordinate his division's tasks with those of other divisions has no qualification to be a manager."

The second thing is to devise a solid educational plan which is applied to the entire company. Emphasis alone is not sufficient. In the "Program to Improve Middle Management's Ability" which was conducted by Toyota Motors a number of years ago, there was this one provision: A division manager must register an item which he considers to be the most important one among all items in his annual policy, and report to the top every six months concerning its progress and results. In most instances, division managers selected tasks which had bearing on coordination with other divisions. This educational program was conducted over a two-year period—and during that time, all division managers were able to enhance their ability for interdivisional coordination.

The third point is for a superior officer to educate actively his subordinates through on-the-job training. At our regularly scheduled division managers' meetings, I stress the importance of interdivisional coordination. I love to hear suggestions from my division managers "to improve coordination between divisions." Knowing that, they respond positively and make many valuable suggestions.

The above is the gist of what I do. Now, changing the subject somewhat, I want to discuss the issue of "not making an enemy when you become a division manager."

I was an instructor at another company when I heard from one of its division managers: "The head of the division with which I must coordinate my work is a very difficult man to deal with. Our chemistries just do not mix, and it's not easy to talk with him."

This is a matter of human relations. The company suffers when a division manager behaves in this manner, but it must still find a way to resolve this thorny issue. Once a person becomes a division manager, he cannot have an enemy or a person whom he has difficulty dealing with. In other words, such a person must not be promoted to be a division head. But once he becomes one, there is very little the company can do. It is up to the division manager to engage in self-cultivation to eliminate these difficulties. Do not dismiss it as a case of personality conflict. A manager must be able to transcend human relations problems through his own effort for the good of the company.

III. Everyone Speaks

At circle meetings, there are some people who say that they are merely attending, and refuse to say a word. "All I have to do is to sit through the meeting" is not a good attitude for anyone to have. He can never feel that he has been part of the meeting, and his ability cannot improve.

To cope with this problem, from the time I first became a plant manager, I have been consistently emphasizing "everyone speaks" at all meetings. Toyoda Gosei adopted the phrase "everyone speaks" as one of its annual slogans for the year 1983, which was the first full year I served as its president.

Reproduced below are five examples of my endeavor toward "everyone speaks."

The first deals with the time when we establish our annual policy. I make the practice of consulting with my subordinates on all important matters affecting the future of the company. I may set certain goals and general guidelines, but I know full well that it is my subordinates who must implement the annual policy, thus their cultivation of the "everyone speaks" attitude becomes critically important. The atmosphere of our sessions is congenial to discussion, and no session goes by without producing many amendments. Here are some examples: "To reach that particular goal, don't you think we must consider X and Y also?"; and "It takes a little longer to implement the second item. Can we wait a little longer before we undertake it?" When everyone's idea is carefully considered before reaching a decision, momentum is created to promote the implementation of our goal. When we reach that stage, I do not have to worry about the details. Everything is expertly done by the division managers.

I utilized the same techniques in promoting greater efficiency in the administrative divisions and technology-related divisions of Toyoda Gosei. When the movement first began in the fall of 1982, all division managers and deputy managers were asked to speak up and discuss matters openly and freely. Consensus was quickly reached in this manner. One of the characteristics of this method was to let each division utilize its own special abilities to the fullest extent and to allow its manager and section chiefs to participate in the deliberations in a creative manner. They were allowed to "do their own things," and as a result discussion among them has always been very lively. This was the ultimate in "everyone speaks." The efficiency movement was begun in this fashion. There was no sense of coercion from the top. Everyone felt that he was promoting a cause he himself had devised—and in a six-month period, we were able to reach the goal of a 10 percent reduction in waste or time expended.

The second thing is "everyone speaks" at regularly scheduled weekly meetings. In addition to our regular agenda, these regular meetings also deal with the issues of fire, industrial accidents and unexpected defectives. Normally, it is a one-to-one conversation where someone makes the report and someone else accepts the report. I have made these occasions into a time for everyone to study prevention of recurrence. For example, if division manager A reports on a certain issue, I ask "Mr. B. What is your opinion?" and "How about you, Mr. C?" I insist on everyone giving his opinion. Not only can we combine our knowledge in devising a solution, but we also can learn from the specific incident under discussion when this approach is utilized.

The third technique is to let "everyone speak" at meetings convened to solve specific problems. Those people who are asked to attend are the people who represent those divisions and offices concerned with the problems under review. A preliminary solution has, of course, been drafted by the division most responsible for the issue. But everyone present—representing various divisions and offices—must make his contribution. There may be someone present who opposes the suggested solution but says nothing. To let the meeting proceed without everyone speaking can lead to misjudgment.

The fourth technique is "everyone speaking" at QC circles. Frequently cited in measuring the effectiveness of QC circle activities are the number of meetings held, and the rate of attendance. I suggest that another yardstick be added. That is the rate of participation in discussion.

The fifth technique is to let "everyone speak" at informal gatherings. There are different types of informal gatherings, such as those for subsection chiefs or for engineers. Even in these types of gatherings, I promote "everyone speaks," to let everyone have a better sense of participation. If there are 20 people in a two-hour meeting, a little advance planning will insure that everyone is given an opportunity to say something at that gathering.

IV. There Is a Reason for Not Scolding

After finishing college, I worked in an arsenal for a while. The facilities for which I was responsible malfunctioned one day, and it was due to my fault. If found out by my superior officer, all hell would break loose. I decided to remain silent and asked a fellow officer who knew about it: "Keep it quiet, will you? When you are in trouble, I will, of course, say nothing." It was a pact of mutual assistance, so to speak, and I took temporary corrective measures to cover up my mistakes.

I thought to myself then: "If only I was sure that I would not be reprimanded severely, I would have implemented basic corrective measures which would have avoided recurrence. When I have subordinates of my own, I will never scold them." More than 30 years have passed since that time, and I have overseen numerous subordinates of my own. During this entire period, I have never scolded any of my subordinates.

"What, you have never scolded your subordinates?" Some people may feel that this is proof positive of my lax manner of management and inability to teach. This is not so. I believe that "people are not gods and they are bound to make mistakes no matter how hard they try. There is no benefit in assessing responsibility for committing errors. It is better to clarify the facts and work toward prevention of recurrence." I check very carefully to see if my subordinates submit their plans for prevention of recurrence on time. My reputation among my subordinates is that I do not scold, but when it comes to work I am very demanding.

Let me share with you my experience with "not scolding when mistakes occur." When we gather to establish our annual policy, we begin by looking back at the performance of the past 12-month period. If a person has been scolded by his superior, he is not likely to be candid, reflective or able to examine himself carefully. It is rare for anyone to have a record of implementing everything in the way he had initially planned and obtaining the results expected. Mistakes and failures are bound to occur along the way. If they are not candidly stated, then the goals which we set for the following year cannot be appropriate ones.

For example, a division manager may state in an abstract manner: "We need to do a little better in handling our meetings." It is not clear what has gone wrong and no appropriate measures can be taken. What he should have said candidly is: "The rate of attendance is good, but the rate of participation in discussion is poor."

In our day-to-day operations, I always tell my people that they must "have ears to listen to the mistakes committed by their subordinates." It is always embarrassing to admit one's own mistakes, but it is important to create an atmosphere which is conducive to making a report of mistakes committed by workers. If a superior raises his voice and shouts, his subordinate will think twice before coming to him.

In Chapter 6, there are a number of examples taken from Toyoda Gosei showing how products not meeting our standards are uncovered. All of these examples are known to us, because our supervisors have been willing to report to us their own mistakes. We can compile examples of our mistakes for future reference, because we have steadfastly abided by our policy of "having ears to listen to the mistakes committed by our subordinates."

Caution must be exercised in disciplining employees. About nine years ago, a parts manufacturer delivered poor quality parts to us. I called the president of the firm and received this response: "We are still investigating, but as soon as we know what has happened you will receive our report. As for the person or persons responsible for this mistake, we are planning to convene our disciplinary board to look into the matter." This last part of his response bothered me, and I called him back immediately. "If the mistake is committed deliberately, the person(s) responsible, of course, must be punished," I said to the president. "But most of those unexpected defectives are caused by an accidental miss. If workers are punished for an accidental miss, their tendency is to cover up any and all mistakes which may occur at the workplace. Supervisors, sympathetic to their workers, will subtly distort the facts to make sure that those workers responsible for the mistake will not face disciplinary action. You gain nothing by convening the disciplinary board."

"One punishment deters 100 similar offenses," says a proverb. It may be valid for preventing murder or other serious crimes. But it is not an appropriate principle to follow in the workplace, where prevention of recurrence must be promoted in a different manner.

V. Try Harder When You Teach, if the Other Party Does Not Understand

Have you ever encountered a situation where a speaker repeats himself over and over again without getting his points across? If the audience cannot understand him, he must change his method of presentation. What is needed is an extra effort. There are some people who say: "I am willing to work out the problems connected with my work, but I do not want to spend time worrying about how to present its contents to others."

In a company, no one can accomplish his work alone. He must explain to others what he is doing and obtain their cooperation. If they can understand only one-half of what he is saying, then their eventual cooperation will become only one-half as effective.

A number of years ago, I was transferred to a new position. In order to get a general idea of what this new position was about, I asked each of the divisions under me to brief me. One of the division managers used so many technical terms while briefing me that I could not understand what he was saying. It is not uncommon for a speaker to think that whatever he knows, the other party can understand. Obviously my speaker was no exception. After his presentation, I cautioned the speaker: "When speaking to nonspecialists like me, please use the language which nonspecialists can understand." I am happy to report that the speaker and his division are today known for the clarity of their presentation. They have done their homework well.

When I speak, I am often complimented: "We did not realize that two hours had passed. Your speech was easy to understand and yet forceful." I put my utmost emphasis on making my speech "easy to understand and yet forceful." I worry about my own presentation and spend a lot of time making improvements on it. Let me illustrate a number of examples.

My first device is the use of blackboards. A speech is supposed to be heard, but I insist on being observed as well as heard. I use two blackboards concurrently. I write my topics down on the first blackboard to the left under the headings of chapters 1 and 2 and the like. The second blackboard to the right is used to draw a graph or illustration while speaking. When a chapter is completed, everything is erased except the topic. This is to let the audience know that the topic is completed.

A second tool I employ is the use of actual examples. I normally select examples with which the audience can identify. For supervisors from the workplace, I cite examples from the workplace. For office workers, I cite examples from different offices. I skip all the unnecessary details. It is better to say that "there was a blaze in the electrostatic coating process at Factory A" than to say that "at the small electrostatic coating process of the twelfth section of the coating department of the first product division of Factory A, there was a blaze." In this case, precision is not a virtue. It simply makes it more difficult for people from other companies to know what you are saying.

A third helpful aid is to use a conversational style and utilize freely all gestures which are appropriate. In this respect, I imitate the style of the traditional Japanese raconteur (*rakugo*). The *rakugo* raconteur is seated when he performs—but in my case, I remain standing and walk around left to right about 10 meters in each direction while talking, performing and explaining. It is easier for the audience when the speaker does this. I use plain language and avoid those familiar phrases which do not convey precise meanings.

The fourth device calls for checking the facilities available at the meeting place. Among the items which I check are: Can everyone read the last line on the two blackboards? Do the lectern and various flower arrangements stand in the way? Will the smoke from cigarettes make the room's air stale? Can the room temperature be controlled? Does the microphone work?

When the time comes for me to deliver my speech, I have a simple evaluative criterion: "In an audience of 100, if more than three persons fall asleep, then the speech is a failure."

VI. Send Out Your Best Subordinates for Rotation

In a long-range education program, there is nothing greater than a well-run rotation program for the employees. When the president says, "Let us do our best to promote rotation," no one disagrees. However, this is one program for which there is no stronger agreement in principle, but which is matched by an equally strong opposition for its individual implementation.

I maintain the position that we must "send out our best and brightest for rotation." The following words of mine express the same sentiment: "Let us send someone who will be appreciated by the receiving end," and "Let us send someone who is nominated or requested by the other party."

The foremost consideration in rotation is the long-range education of the employees so affected. If they are not worthy, then there is no point in educating them, since the utility of rotation may not be felt until 10 or 20 years later.

The second consideration in rotation is to supply key personnel for the company's important projects, such as new projects or expanded projects. We must select employees who can handle these important responsibilities. That is why I say that we must send someone who will be "appreciated by the receiving end" or "nominated or requested by the other party."

In companies where there is strong resistance to implementing a good rotation policy, division managers often send people who cannot do work in their own divisions. This practice defeats the objectives set forth in the first and second considerations cited above. To companies which allow such a practice, I have this to say: "Those managers who insist on retaining their best workers indefinitely are fools. Companies which allow such a practice are also fools, and they deserve each other."

This is an aside. Whenever someone is newly placed under my supervision, I say to him: "Remain with me for three or four years and learn everything you can. Once you master the work here, I am going to let you be rotated to another workplace. On the other hand, if you cannot master everything in four years, I plan to keep you here as long as necessary."

Every year, I ask my subordinates to set their own annual goals. In this way, they know how far they have progressed, and can report to their superiors about their own progress as well. There are far too many people who feel that they come to work in order to obtain their salaries or wages. I choose to think that they come to learn by tackling actual problems. Therefore, if someone comes to me and reports that he has completed a year of work without incident, I am extremely dissatisfied. I want him to be able to say to me: "This past year, I was assigned to this task. Through this work, my ability has improved this much."

VII. A Command Without a Deadline Is Not a Command

There is a saying that "a command without a set date is not a command." Unless a deadline is set, no one knows when that task must be completed. Is the task to be completed by tomorrow, by next week, by next month or by next year? Without a deadline, to engage in a task or not becomes a question. The one who has given the command may forget it, and he may not press for its completion.

I used to give instructions to my subordinates by reminding myself that "a command without a deadline is not a command." But occasionally I would forget to set a deadline and created a certain confusion. In order to discipline myself, one day I declared to all of my subordinates: "If I give a command without a deadline, do not consider it a command."

Thereafter, whenever a command is given, the deadline has been clearly stated. Deadlines are always given to those requests for day-to-day research reports. I also clearly state that "a plan must be submitted by so-and-so date," in all items concerning implementation of measures against defectives.

When we discuss measures against defectives, we include deadlines in the minutes of our discussion. For individualized requests, I ascertain how long it will take to complete each project, and ask my subordinate: "If you think you can complete this project within two weeks, then have the completed report on my desk by Monday, the 5th of next month." As I say these words, I inscribe the date in my notebook. The other party is forced to enter the same date on his schedule.

There is another important issue. That is to prepare a schedule for checking each item contained in the annual policy. Just because these implementation items are contained in the annual policy, it does not mean that they need be checked only once at year's end. In some instances, it is necessary to check everything at the "takeoff" stage. There are some items which must be checked in mid-year. All of these must be determined at the time the annual policy is established. Here I am using the word "schedule" instead of "deadline." This is so, because it is not necessary to establish a precise date or dates to check these items. A targeted month, such as July or August, will suffice. That becomes the deadline for our purpose.

Let us now use the control circle to explain this concept. A schedule must be clearly established for implementing each of the four stages of "plan, do, check and action." It is too late to make this determination if you have already reached the "do" stage. The schedule for checking each of the items must be completed while you are still on your "plan" stage. I wish to recommend this approach to those of you who are interested in proceeding with "policy control." In addition to "planning to establish a checking schedule," if you can also determine the "method of checking" at the same time, so much the better. (See Figure 1–1.)

"Nemoto does not scold, but when it comes to work he is very demanding" is the reputation I have in my own company. I think this is due to the fact that I insist on everyone observing the deadline, and I also check very carefully everything I do.

Figure 1-1: Nemoto Style Control Circle

VIII. Rehearsal Is an Ideal Occasion for Training

To give a report on the occasion of the presidential inspection (or presidential audit, or companywide inspection; these words are used interchangeably), or to make a presentation at a QC conference is a good way to conclude QC promotion activities. It also has great educational value.

Everyone agrees with the importance of making presentations as described above, but seldom does one find anyone emphasizing the importance of rehearsal which is required to prepare for these events. "I don't have to learn how to speak well in public, and I don't have time," is often the excuse given by some in avoiding a rehearsal. Be that as it may, I firmly believe that rehearsal provides an ideal opportunity for training.

I have fully utilized rehearsal to provide training in the following two areas.

The first area concerns QC itself.

In my company, basic ideas concerning QC and its basic methods are taught to everyone—but as to the application of QC in an actual work situation, not enough training has been given.

If we hear a QC story of how improvements are made, we can immediately know the strengths and weaknesses of the person making the presentation. In such a case, it is easy to give him additional guidance by concentrating on a few important issues.

The second area is concerned with both the method of preparing materials and the method of presentation.

Inadequacies are even more discernible in this area than in the first one. At our regularly scheduled QC meetings, or at the place where decisions can be rendered individually, appropriate questions can cover for the lack of adequate materials or explanation. This is not possible at the presidential inspection or at a QC conference where time is at a premium. If a problem is not adequately explained, it cannot be rectified with a well-placed question. Listeners may leave the meeting without ever receiving a clear picture of what has been said.

It is not good to leave listeners in the dark. This is the reason why I insist on utilizing the rehearsal as an occasion for training, and I usually include my middle managers in this training program.

The following is my checklist for the rehearsal:

(1) Are the contents easily understood? Is the document written with a specific audience in mind.

Is the audience a group of specialists or nonspecialists? The manner of presentation naturally must be geared to the type of audience one has. Are the people in the audience mathematically inclined or not? That factor must always be taken into account.

(2) Is the print large enough for older people in attendance. How well are graphs and charts integrated to the text? Do you use boldface to put emphasis on important issues?

The audience for middle management is often primarily made up of those who are older. So it is best to choose a larger size type when preparing a written report for them. If too much is written on a page in small print, they may lose interest in reading it from the outset.

(3) Do the graphs and charts say what you want them to convey? Is the manner in which you are rounding off numbers appropriate?

Graphs and charts are supposed to help your audience understand what you want to say. If you get a question like the following, then it is clear that you have not done your job well: "Where shall I look in this chart to know what you are saying?" You may provide accurate and detailed figures. But they can become too cumbersome. It is necessary to round them off at the point you think is appropriate for understanding.

(4) In preparing your materials, have you thought of coordinating them with the number of minutes it takes to make your presentation?

At a QC conference or presidential audit, each presentation is confined to 10 or 15 minutes. Your source materials must be consistent with the time frame given to you. My rule of thumb is for a 10-minute presentation, all accompanying materials must be printed on one double letter size sheet of paper (approximately $16\frac{1}{2} \times 11\frac{3}{4}$ inches).

(5) Are the "speed of delivery," "strength of voice" and "clarity of word or phrase ending" appropriate?

None of these can be corrected in one or two sessions. They stem largely from the speaker's own personality and lifetime habits. If someone has a peculiar habit which inhibits good delivery, his superior must give him special training to correct it.

(6) Are you making sure that the "lost-child syndrome" does not occur?

If the audience does not know which point is being explained, that phenomenon is called "becoming a lost child" at Toyota. In order not to create this lost-child syndrome, I suggest the following:

a. In making your presentation, follow as closely as you can the order given in your accompanying material.

b. When you skip a certain item, say so clearly. When you return to the original item, again clearly so state.

c. If you add something which is not on the accompanying material, say: "This is not included in the accompanying material, but . . ."

(7) When charts and graphs are hung in front of the audience, consider carefully how you place yourself, how you walk and how you use your pointing stick.

IX. Inspection Itself Is a Failure When Top Management Takes No Action

When I serve as an instructor for our affiliated companies, I often pose my questions this way: "Have you ever engaged in a companywide inspection? What is its overall effect? What are the actions you have to take as the top manager? What actions do you have in store for your company?"

This is an answer I received from the president of an affiliated company: "My overall assessment is so-so. However, Plant B has the worst record, with its foremen and plant manager showing the lowest level of attainment. I told them to shape up." But does the president's responsibility end when he tells his subordinates to shape up?

Why does Plant B show a lower level of attainment? There is a need to investigate the factors causing it and take action. If there are not enough personnel to handle the QC promotion program at Plant B, a companywide system of assisting Plant B must be created. For example, one staff member from the QC promotion office and the division of quality assurance may be stationed at Plant B on a regular basis to assist the plant manager. If it is found that more study of QC is needed, the frequency of visits by outside QC instructors to Plant B may be increased. Or the company may decide to hold its regularly scheduled meetings of the Control Chart Study Group at Plant B. Or some of the section chiefs may be transferred elsewhere. There are always some concrete steps which the company can take.

If there is a will, the top management can take many appropriate actions. When it takes no action and tells the employees to shape up by saying "do your best," then it has failed in discharging its responsibility to the company. The companywide inspection itself becomes a failure.

Of course, some of the measures which top management intends to take cannot be made public beforehand. These measures include transferring section chiefs and changing the organizational structure. They, of course, must be known only to top management until the time comes for regular reshuffling. Thus many employees may not realize that transfers are actually part of the actions taken in response to the companywide inspection.

X. Creating an Opportunity to Be Heard by the Top: Ask "What Can I Do for You?"

We create opportunities for employee opinions to be heard by top management when introducing QC. For want of a better term, we call this system "top hearing." In its function, it is not different from the companywide inspection or presidential audit, but it is an opportunity to be heard by the top management during the initial stage of QC introduction and it serves our purpose far better. By its nature it is not intended to be a formal presentation.

"Top hearing" usually takes place within the first or second year of QC's introduction to the company. Those who are making the presentations and those who are listening to them are still not quite used to QC. So it is best not to discuss something which is too difficult or complicated.

When you initiate a program of "top hearing," please observe the following:

(1) Once you decide to hold the meeting, stick to the original schedule.

Abide by what you have promised. If top management tells its subordinates that it is too busy for a particular meeting and keeps on extending the date, the subordinates will lose all interest. Those who want to have a chance to be heard have studied hard preparing for it. Don't disappoint them.

(2) Listen to the process as well as to the results.

Some top managers may say: "The results sound good, I don't have to hear any more," or "The results have been bad, yet they insist on saying they have done this and that. I don't like to hear something resembling an apology or excuse." Why is it that the company is promoting QC? Knowing the process is what QC is about. Top management must always be ready to listen to the countermeasures adopted and how they are implemented.

When you keep on telling your employees "to do your best," you may receive some reports in return saying that they are doing a little better. Don't be satisfied with such "pat" general remarks. Aside from "doing their best," what concrete steps have they taken toward improvement? Be sure to ask them.

(3) Top management must ask of the presenters: "Is there anything I can do for you?"

As discussed earlier, if top management fails to take action after the completion of an inspection, then the inspection itself must be judged a failure. After asking "Is there anything I can do for you?" and the presenters make only a few suggestions, then top management can at least take one specific action. It may be a small move—but the posture itself, or the willingness itself, is what counts.

Tell the people who are making the presentation ahead of time that you will be asking them if there are things you can do for them at the meeting. Then they can come prepared to respond to your question.

There used to be a time when I asked everyone individually: "At this stage, is there anything I can do for you?" After a while everyone got used to that question. So anticipating the question, they began noting their requests on their supporting materials ahead of time. For most people, there is at least one item for which they need my help. It is neatly noted between the columns on "remaining problems" and "how to proceed in the future." Some people simply write: "As long as we can get cooperation from the division next to us, we can accomplish the task without having to ask assistance from the top. But we believe we can do our work better if the top knows about this."

This is an aside. A president of one of our sales organizations used this phrase: "Is there anything I can do for you?" Everyone present was surprised but pleased. It was the first time ever that the president spoke to his section chiefs and dealers in this fashion. That "top hearing" meeting turned into a convivial session, and all the dealers present decided that QC was a good thing for them!

2

Efficiency in Administrative Divisions and Technology-Related Divisions

It has been more than 20 years since I first began studying total quality control (TQC). As a middle manager, and then as a top ranking manager, I have always grappled with difficult problems with the aid of TQC. One of the first important tasks I undertook after becoming president of Toyoda Gosei was "making our administrative divisions and technology-related divisions more efficient." In this chapter I should like to discuss what I have done to promote efficiency and how I felt about it as the chief operating officer. I also would like to discuss the cooperation I have received on a companywide scale, and some intermediate results and tasks still remaining.

I should be grateful if, in reading this chapter, you could go beyond the issue of promoting efficiency to discover TQC's role in formulating top management's attitude and strategy toward issues.

I. Why Did We Decide to Promote Efficiency?

First, let me explain the background which led to the adoption of our policy in quest of efficiency.

Reshuffling Personnel to Strengthen Important Divisions

The world was lapsing into a period of low growth, but the company acted as if the prior period of high growth would never end when it made allocation of its resources. As a result, in the first half of 1982, for each successive month, we experienced a slight decrease in sales and a sharp drop in profits.

It would be easy to blame the worldwide "recession" for the company's less-than-adequate performance. But that was not the way I wanted to approach the issue. I felt that a very important structural problem was not made apparent in our company.

We made an exhaustive analysis of our structure. Our conclusion was that we should reshuffle our human resources as one measure of arresting lethargic tendencies. There are two important divisions within our company. They are the division of technology development and the marketing division. We decided to shift some of our personnel to these two divisions without going through the route of hiring new employees. Qualitatively speaking, new employees would not be as satisfactory, and training them would take too much time. Therefore, we felt that we could select people from our other administrative and technology-related divisions to be reassigned to these two divisions.

Improving Productivity in the Administrative and Technology-Related Divisions

Another reason was productivity.

Toyoda Gosei has been known as one of the top-ranked companies in productivity in the industry. But this was true only with regards to our manufacturing sector. Compared to the workplace, I felt that productivity of our administrative divisions was below par. There was no exact yardstick to measure the productivity of administrative divisions, and we were not able to say how well or how poorly we were doing compared to other companies. But subjectively, I could see room for substantial improvement.

Our books were already showing less receipts and less profits. So the problem could not be ignored. I decided to start the process of improvement immediately.

As the two factors coalesced into one, it became a rather powerful force in promoting our movement for efficiency.

Our First Steps

Efficiency for administrative and technology-related divisions is often touted in principle but abused in practice. Each of the divisions affected may agree with the goals set by the company president, but oppose any measures which may affect the division. For example, when a division is asked to name some of its best people for rotation to be reassigned to other divisions, its enthusiastic "support" might suddenly turn into undisguised opposition. To prevent this from happening, we took a number of steps from the outset. They are discussed below.

I became president of Toyoda Gosei in October of 1982. Prior to that, for a two-year period, I served as a part-time director in charge of enhancing the managerial capabilities of its middle management. In July of 1982, I knew unofficially that I was to be named the company's president. At that juncture, I began my preparation by first consulting with Mr. Sohei Kato (its president). I then contacted representatives from all divisions in the company and explained to them the purpose of the movement we were about to launch.

The gist of my talk could be summarized by the following three items:

(1) Making our company more efficient does not mean engaging in "management through reduction in quantity" which always has a negative connotation. An important task for this movement is to find a way of surviving and growing in a period of zero growth. One positive aspect of our movement is to nurture human resources capable of developing new products and opening new needs and markets.

(2) Therefore we must use the most rigorous selection process to identify the most capable people and place them on rotation.

(3) The selection process for human resources must follow the thinking of the Toyota production system and be developed accordingly. The Toyota production system engages in a massive "clean-up operation" to eliminate all types of waste. It looks on issues such as "Can this operation be eliminated?" "Can this process be simplified?" "Can the separate processes be combined?" and "Can the combined processes be simplified?" On the matter of rotation, it does not ask if people can be withdrawn from some existing divisions. Instead, it simply removes people, and lets the affected divisions cope without them. In so doing, new ideas are bound to surface. These two key points—elimination of waste and withdrawal of workers—must always be kept in mind when discussing the Toyota production system.

II. Efficiency Target

I decided to set our efficiency target at 30 percent for a 20 month period.

In setting a target, usually the higher it is, the better it is. As the president, I would like to have stated that there should be an increase in efficiency of 50 percent within a two-year period. If the purpose is merely to challenge the employees, it would be fine to set a 50 percent target. But it lacks persuasiveness. So I began my search for a figure which would be realistic and yet challenging enough as a target to be met. I approached the issue from the following two angles.

The first was our relationship with the manufacturing divisions' efficiency target. These manufacturing divisions normally set as their target "an increase of 10 percent annually in productivity." There were times when they attained only an increase of 8 or 9 percent. But as the target, 10 percent was set to challenge the workers at all times. The administrative divisions so far had done nothing, and there was plenty of room for improvement. If they would set as their target an increase of 10 percent during the first year, and 20 percent during the second year of the two-year period, the workplace would simply laugh at them. The target had to be set high enough to show their resolve in meeting the challenge of efficiency.

The second angle came directly from my own personal experience. During the time I was with Toyota Motors, I had an opportunity to lead a movement for efficiency in the offices for two years. In this movement, those who were classified as class A offices raised their efficiency by 30 to 40 percent during a two-year period. How well their record compared with those of other companies, I did not know. But as a performance record of our own, it was persuasive.

My conclusion was that we could attain an increase in efficiency of 20 percent a year and 40 percent in two years. At the time we began our movement at Toyoda Gosei, the first fiscal year (Toyoda Gosei's fiscal year begins on May 1) was already three months past, having gone through May, June and July. So I set the target for our first fiscal year at 10 percent, and 20 percent for the next fiscal year, or a total of 30 percent. During the initial year, the months of July and August were spent in preparation. The movement did not officially begin until the first of September, leaving only eight months for the remainder of fiscal 1983. Adding the 12 months for the next fiscal year, we had a total of 20 months to meet our target.

The Meaning of the Figure 30 Percent

What does it mean to attain an increase in efficiency of 30 percent? It means one thing when the workload increases, and another thing when the workload does not increase. The figure of 30 percent may be the same, but the degree of difficulty in attaining it is not.

Let us assume that there is a job which once required 10 people. The workload has been increased by 30 percent, but the same number of people are engaged in completing the job. In this case, we can say that the efficiency has been increased by 30 percent.

In another instance, an amount of work which once required 10 people has remained the same, but through improvement the identical amount of work is completed by seven people. In other words, three people have been withdrawn from the work force. This also represents an increase of 30 percent in efficiency.

Both of these instances represent an increase in efficiency of 30 percent, and as such are to be commended. But when the degree of difficulty is taken into account, the latter is much harder to accomplish. To withdraw three people does not mean that the work done by them suddenly disappears. In rare instances their jobs may be eliminated. But in most other cases, job roles are simplified, or certain jobs are combined with the jobs of others, automated or made less cumbersome to handle. The jobs performed by the withdrawn three workers are performed and shared by the remaining seven. The seven have to learn new jobs which they have not done before. In short, they must become versatile.

At Toyoda Gosei, we chose the latter and more difficult approach. We wanted to improve the jobs done by 10 workers and let seven workers handle the same workload. The remaining three are to be withdrawn and then reassigned to more pressing positions in other divisions.

Marketing and Technology Divisions Are Also Objects of the Efficiency Movement

Generally speaking, when the target is established, the objects or factors that will be focused on are also identified. However, in the present instance, there was a set of special circumstances that had to be dealt with first which must be explained.

When we speak of administrative divisions, at the company headquarters, they normally include those divisions with responsibilities over personnel, general affairs, accounting, quality assurance and production management. At plants, the term refers to the departments of general engineering and inspection. Generally, marketing and technology divisions are not included in this category. At Toyoda Gosei, we included these two divisions in the category of administrative divisions and made them both equal objects of our efficiency movement. It was an unusual approach, and there were two compelling reasons for doing so.

The first reason was that while from the point of view of the company as a whole, marketing and technology divisions required strengthening, they themselves could stand some improvement in many of their work procedures. People in technology development do not spend their entire working day just thinking. Their work includes seeking information and making experimental models. The methods of doing these things could be improved. Similarly, many areas of work of those people who draft graphs and charts could also be improved.

I decided to seek improvement in these areas and transfer those people who were no longer needed in these divisions to perform even more important functions.

The second reason involved preventing people who had been transferred from other divisions to marketing and technology from commenting: "How inefficient can these people be? In our previous divisions, we worked to the limit of our ability in order to attain the highest efficiency. Here they are working in a well-protected greenhouse atmosphere. We came here ready to help, but this is certainly disappointing. I wonder what Mr. Nemoto had in mind? Is he not worried about the overall balance of our company?" I, of course, could not allow this to happen.

Therefore, without exception, marketing and technology divisions were included and focused upon in our efficiency promotion movement. It was not always necessary to remove and reassign those excess people resulting from the movement to other divisions. They could remain in their own division to engage in either developing new technology or a new market.

III. Methods of Promoting the Efficiency Movement

As you may have observed, I have promoted this efficiency movement with techniques learned from TQC. We have included this movement as part of our policy control, and the movement itself has been supported by the participation of all members.

Issues such as efficiency require six months, one year or even two years to implement. When they require a long-term commitment, I insist that such issues be included and clearly stated in our annual policy statement. And when an issue is a new one, I spare no effort in obtaining a consensus by engaging in extensive preliminary discussions.

When we discuss our company's policy, I invite our middle management to participate in its deliberation fully. And depending on the themes selected, I may even invite all affected employees to participate thoroughly in the deliberation. Efficiency is one of the most important themes that any company can have, and it requires participation by all affected employees. This view is consistent with TQC's basic notion of "respect for humanity." People perform better in implementing plans if they have had a part in devising them. Their cooperation contributes greatly to the success of such plans.

First Point to Consider: "Start from Elimination of Waste"

In promoting efficiency, companies can establish three approaches. Perhaps the word "approaches" is not quite appropriate, so I shall use the term "points to consider."

The first point to consider is "start from the elimination of waste." There are many people in administrative divisions who equate efficiency with office automation, and there are many in technology-related divisions who equate efficiency with computer-aided design (CAD). That is a simplistic view. I believe that there is something which must be done before that. That is elimination of all types of waste.

There are some people who utilize their computers to do the kind of work which no longer needs to be done. If it is performed as their own hobby, that is perfectly fine, but it must not be done on company time. These people may say that "there is not a single item of work which is wasted." But the more we think about it, the more we become aware of many types of work which need not be done. At a certain time in the past, there might have been a certain meaning to a particular job, but today there is no justification for its existence.

Let me cite an example. A few years back there was a female worker in the office whose responsibility included transcribing the contents of payment vouchers and receiving slips into a notebook. The worker came to me and said: "I inherited this work from my predecessor. I have been on this job for two years and no one has ever asked to see the notebook. If I stop doing this work, I can save 20 hours each month." In suggesting that this work be eliminated, she also mentioned that all the chits were kept in the document room, and any necessary information could be obtained within 30 minutes. If the work had not been utilized for two years, there was certainly no justification for its continuation, especially when there was another way of finding the required information.

Here is another and more recent example at Toyoda Gosei. There was a female worker in the Personnel Department whose responsibility included handling of suggestions submitted. Every month, she stamped over 2,000 suggestions to indicate at what time and date they were received. Her own suggestion was that this practice be eliminated. The receiving stamp idea originated with the notion that if there were multiple suggestions on the same matter, the one which was first submitted should receive the recognition. (It is the practice of the National Patent Office, incidentally.) But there was not a single case in which this had occurred. By eliminating this practice, the worker could save eight hours each month.

Incidents like the above abound. I can fill a chapter with actual examples. In trying to solve problems similar to the ones just discussed, we ask the following questions: "Is there any work that is being done which is really not necessary?" "Can the work procedure be simplified?" "Is there a better way of doing it?" "What will happen if we change or adjust our tools?"

Management must then take the next logical step and bunch together the hours saved to make it possible for the division to withdraw a worker. To "withdraw workers" and do it thoroughly is one of the characteristics of the Toyota production system.

In the current drive for efficiency, the first step is to withdraw workers as suggested by the Toyota production system. Only then can we proceed to the next step of office automation and the use of CAD.

Second Point to Consider: "From Above and Below"

Who initiates suggestions and who implements them? From the standpoint of promoting efficiency in administrative divisions, there are three different approaches.

The first is for the top to initiate improvement plans and impose them on subordinates. The second is for the top to encourage or even force the subordinates to initiate plans while confining its own role to that of assembling the plans submitted. The third is to let both the top and the subordinates initiate plans and implement them. In the current drive at Toyoda Gosei, I stress the need for participation "from above and below," as outlined in the third option above. The willingness to engage in efficiency improvement must be shared companywide.

In most administrative divisions, seldom does a division manager or section chief know how any one of his subordinates handles his day-to-day work. Ask a question of a division manager: "Can you find any waste in the routine work performed by your female workers?" The answer you receive is likely to be as follows: "Well, I haven't really looked into the work of female workers. I don't know." Therefore it is important to ask each and every one of the workers to think about his own work routine. The manager's function is to accept suggestions, coordinate them and see to it that these suggestions are implemented. Small group activities, such as QC circles and QC groups, are helpful in fostering the workers' willingness for improvement.

When there are many suggestions, some of them may contain problems which cannot be solved within the division. For example, on matters relating to keeping books and vouchers and chits, coordination with other divisions often becomes necessary. A female worker who has written such a suggestion cannot do the negotiations all by herself. Matters like this must be handled by her superior. If a division manager or section chief shows his willingness to get involved in solving problems, he can expect enthusiastic responses from his subordinates toward improvement. Normally, the manager retains the most difficult problems for himself and organizes teams to handle the next most difficult ones. Teams can also be empowered to negotiate with other divisions.

So far, we have been discussing discovery of waste from the perspectives of individuals or divisions and sections. There are improvement plans which must be seen from the overall perspective of the company. We must also be concerned with the problem of how to make the entire company more efficient. In situations like this, subordinates are not well suited to make suggestions. Top management must be the one to be concerned with this issue. Problems which they must consider may include "a review of our receiving and delivery system, and a possible change in our organization" or "uniformity in our office automation machines."

By having suggestions come "from above and below," and by coordinating the two, momentum toward improvement can be created.

Third Point to Consider: "Freedom in Selecting a Method of Implementation"

Normally when a company establishes a policy, the method of its implementation is set by the company, and each division must follow it. In the case of our current drive for efficiency, the practice has been that "each division is to consider its own special attributes and establish its own method of implementation. Division directors and section chiefs are encouraged to deal with this issue creatively and in their own way."

Why did I say these things? I was aware that the goal of "making our division efficient in order to withdraw some key people from the work force" was not going to be a popular one. The president might wish to do his best in bringing about its success, but the rest may not follow his lead willingly. Thus I decided to allow as much room as possible for middle management to maneuver. I told them to "consider their divisions' special attributes and be creative." They could not imitate what other divisions were doing. Naturally the division manager and his section chiefs would have to get together to study the pending issues. In such meetings, I suspect that the following points were discussed:

1. Is there a need to establish a separate division-wide organization to promote efficiency?

2. What types of projects require direct participation by the division manager and section chiefs? In what areas? And in what way?

3. Is it necessary to organize teams using the themes proposed for the movement?

4. What can we do to encourage suggestions from our subordinates? What kind of system should be established to receive these suggestions?

5. Is it wise to establish QC circles and QC groups?

6. How often shall we hold study meetings and meetings for presentation of improvement ideas?

7. How do we teach some of the techniques and methods (e. g., the Toyota production system and office automation)?

8. What method can we use in withdrawing personnel from our work force? How do we train our workers in versatility?

As they discussed these issues, each of these divisions determined its own method for promoting efficiency. As they progressed in this fashion, there was no longer a sense of being forced to do something. This attitude became a very positive force in helping us promote the movement.

IV. Conditions at Our Takeoff Stage

At the end of September, 1982, I confirmed conditions at the takeoff stage in each of the divisions. The personnel division served as the secretariat for the movement. I followed a schedule provided by the secretariat and examined divisions one by one. My impression at that time was that each of these divisions understood my intent clearly and organized an implementation method different from each other, and yet significant in its own way. I was convinced that "we could attain the 30 percent increase in efficiency as initially planned."

Let me show you one of the more unusual methods of implementation. At one of the divisions, before the program was going to start, one person was withdrawn from each of the sections. The work of the person withdrawn was then shared by the remaining members of the section.

For those people who were left behind, they had to handle their normal workload plus part of the work of the person withdrawn. It was not an easy task. But as they suffered through this shock, many improvement plans were proposed.

Among the plans recommended, those which could be implemented within the division were quickly put into practice. But there were some which called for negotiation with other divisions. Normally, it is the responsibility of the manager to engage in the task of negotiating. However, at this division, the task was given to a team of five persons withdrawn from the five sections in the division. They constituted the improvement promotion team for the division. When problems were too difficult even for this team to handle, the division manager would come to their rescue.

Those five who were withdrawn were the best members of their own sections. Joining the team provided them with an opportunity to study conditions existing in other divisions and learn about the interrelatedness of the divisions. Sooner or later, these people are destined to leave their present positions for more challenging activities, such as development of new markets.

V. Interim Inspection of March 1983

I made an interim inspection of each division in March of 1983 to see how its efficiency promotion had been progressing in the past one-half year period. Every division had its own unique system of TQC promotion and the results had been encouraging. Our overall goal was to raise efficiency by 10 percent (by withdrawing 131 workers). But the actual records showed an attainment of 11.7 percent (or 147 workers withdrawn) which was much better than expected. The pie chart below provides further information on this matter.

VI. Problems Remaining and How to Proceed in the Future

Figure 2–1 indicates the results of the first fiscal year. Of the three categories contained in the chart, the goal of "withdrawing workers" is attained by (A) attrition, not hiring to replace retirees, and (B) transfer to other divisions. However, care must be taken in evaluating the results contained in the remainder (C). There it is claimed that 52 workers were either transferred to other activities within the division or utilized to reduce overtime. In obtaining this figure, they might have simply added the hours saved and expressed the total with the equivalent in the number of employees. It might be possible that not a single person was actually withdrawn from the work process. This was our first remaining problem.

As we discussed these issues, there was a request that we adopt a unified view which could be accepted by all. My response was that attainment of efficiency by so many percentage points in itself would not be sufficient, and that our evaluation criterion should be based on "how many people have been withdrawn from the work force." Thus goals for individual divisions for the second fiscal year were restated to emphasize the number of workers removed from the work force, not merely in terms of a 20 percent increase in efficiency. For those division managers who took this challenge seriously but could not actually with-

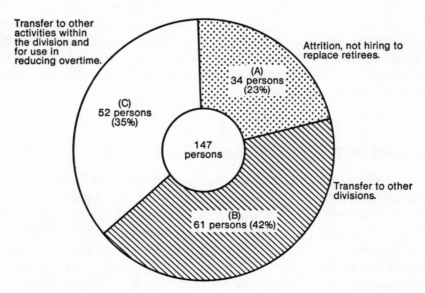

Figure 2-1: Interim Results of Efficiency Movement

draw workers, I allowed them to use another criterion by counting the man-hour reduction attained and totaled them to obtain the equivalent in the number of workers removed.

As I worked closely with these divisions, a few things became clear. Among them was the fact that there was a large number of managers who could not withdraw people from their own workplaces as taught by the Toyota production system.

Nowadays, I am asking each of the divisions to establish its own educational plan separately. As soon as it formulates a plan, I ask to see it. I am putting a lot of emphasis on the technology division. At the first session of its educational program which was to last six months, I gave a two-hour orientation lecture. Thereafter, I have followed their schedule closely to monitor its various activities.

The second problem deals with the issue of placing people in new projects within the same division. Are these new projects really useful

President   [   ]
Managing Director [   ]

CHECKLIST OF NEW PROJECTS _____ DIVISION

Name of Division Manager _____

Name of New Project	Person in Charge	Special Memorandum
1. XYZ project—newly developed	Taro Yamada	Wish to add another person from October, 1983.
2. Joint development project with A Materials Co.	Shiro Kato	Starting June, 1983. Kato plans to be stationed at A Materials Co. in July.
3.		
4.		

Table 2-1: Checklist of New Projects

to the company? The important issues in my mind are: in the case of the technology-related area, that of technical development; and in the case of marketing, development of new markets. We try to pick the right persons to perform these tasks through this movement, yet I am still not certain if our system is working.

To check the results, I am consulting a checklist of new projects as shown in Table 2–1. Important new projects in areas other than technology-related and marketing fields are also included in this checklist. I determine priority for these new projects from a companywide perspective.

The above is my interim report on the efficiency promotion movement conducted by administrative divisions. I hope I have been able to share with you my concerns and problems accurately and candidly.

VII. Questions and Answers

Question 1. What Must Be Done When Implementation Methods Are Not Uniform?

I understand that your personnel division is serving as the secretariat for the entire company in your efficiency movement. But the methods of implementation differ from division to division. You cannot even utilize a single form to record these various activities. How do you handle an administrative headache thus created?

Answer

Normally there is an office of efficiency promotion which receives information from all participating divisions and compiles their reports to transmit them to the president. It is certainly easier for this office to have a unified form which allows it to treat all activities alike in making its own report.

For this project, however, my approach has been that "each division is to consider its own special attributes and establish its own method of implementation. Division directors and section chiefs are encouraged to deal with this issue creatively and in their own way." Thus the methods of implementation differ from one division to another. In the middle of its implementation, we cannot have materials showing how far we have gone overall. It does not really matter if we do not have such materials. All I have to know is how well each division's unique system of implementation is progressing at the time of the six-month inspection. I can then ask if it has reached the goal of attaining a 10 percent increase in efficiency. Some of you may say it is difficult to listen to reports from all the divisions separately. But I enjoy it. I am happiest when I can see enthusiasm in the division managers, and when they reach their targets.

Question 2. How Active Are QC Circles in Technology-Related Divisions?

In one of the actual examples you cited, you mentioned that QC circles are very active in your company. In our company, QC circles are active in the manufacturing divisions but not in the administrative and technology-related divisions. This has been a problem for us. Can you show us how to proceed?

Answer

May I respond to your question by expressing my own opinion, because I receive so many questions very similar to yours at various companies? At the shops, QC circles provide the most ideal opportunity for workers to express their opinions, be they on the subjects of reducing defectives, increasing the yield rate or accident prevention. The meetings are rather enjoyable for circle members, and as for their supervisors, the meetings provide opportunities to be exposed to the opinions of line workers. So they treat these occasions with respect.

In the technology-related divisions, problems similar to those in the workplace are treated as part of their routine work. There are meetings within the working hours which determine the measures to be taken, and these measures are usually implemented. Thus there is very little likelihood of their convening meetings after hours.

Also in the technology-related divisions, in order to raise the level of their own proper techniques, study groups and presentation meetings are organized. If they are to have after-hour meetings, they would prefer meetings of this type. I am in full sympathy with this view.

Under these circumstances, it is not appropriate to suggest that they organize QC circles and actively participate in them in the manner practiced at the workplace. They need something more challenging.

For Toyoda Gosei, I thought in the following terms: "Is there any theme which has not been studied? Can it also be a theme which is suitable for discussion by the technical people at meetings such as QC circles?" My answer was the theme of "efficiency." It was consistent with "man-hour reduction" and "improvement in productivity," themes which were adopted as annual goals in the past for manufacturing workers, which continued to be discussed and studied by middle management and QC circles.

In 1983, "efficiency for technology-related divisions" became part of our annual policy for the first time. I felt that this was an appropriate theme for technology-related people's QC circle activities.

"An increase in efficiency of 30 percent" was an important theme. Middle management had to hold study meetings to exchange ideas with a view to their implementation. They undertook as part of their work assisting QC circle activities, because of the helpful roles QC could perform in the total scheme. With the interest shown by middle management toward this efficiency theme, QC activities were materially strengthened.

As for the hours set aside for circle meetings, they could choose their own. And the names of the circles were also allowed to be freely chosen. They could be "an improvement circle" or "a QC group."

Question 3. Don't You Cause Problems by Withdrawing Workers Ahead of Time?

When we follow the thinking of the Toyota production system and withdraw a worker from a manufacturing process ahead of time, it does not create problems. In doing so, the "line must be stopped" and existing problems become apparent. It allows workers to take action quickly and no major problem will develop. However, in technology-related work, if a worker is withdrawn ahead of time, the remaining people must do his work in addition to their normally assigned work. We fear that these workers may consciously or unconsciously engage in less work. If this happens, there may be difficulty ahead for the company. How do you deal with this?

Answer

After a worker is withdrawn, the remaining employees must do additional work. So if overtime increases temporarily, so be it. But beyond that initial phase, the remaining employees must find ways to improve the manner in which they do their work, and bring overtime down to the level which existed prior to the withdrawal of the specific worker.

In the technology-related field, there is always fear that employees may stop working on a project or simplify it. In so doing they may create greater problems for the future. However, it does not mean that this fear must be pervasive in all types of work handled by the technology-related field. Engineers with experience and with proper techniques can pass judgment on this issue. We cannot, of course, leave this question for newly hired employees to decide.

This is an aside. In the late 1970s when I started "value engineering for equipment and facilities," many similar views were expressed. To wit: "Value engineering for parts which are mass produced poses no problem at all, because prior to its implementation, there are tests conducted and results confirmed. In the case of equipment and facilities, each one is distinct, and value engineering must be implemented without a test or confirmation. There is fear that major problems may surface in the future, and the very notion of value engineering for equipment and facilities is suspect."

But I insisted on going ahead with our VE program. I said to my detractors: "Let us do it. If an engineer with experience and proper techniques determines that there will be no major problem ahead even if we make some mistakes, then there is nothing which prevents us from implementing this program." As we look back, we had some minor problems, but overall the results have been impressive.

We must determine if the action we take will create major problems, but otherwise we must actively promote improvement. In this way, we can bring about improvement in our technology-related field.

Question 4. What Do You Do When a Person Is Not Suitable?

In order to develop new technology and new markets, you are saying that you want to assign people who are withdrawn from other divisions. But suppose they are not suitable, how do you handle this?

Answer

I engage in a triangular trade to obtain the right person. We send a person from Division A to Division B, and get the right person from Division B for the division which is to be strengthened. This will involve a companywide system of rotation, and must be handled by the personnel division.

Question 5. How Often Do You Review Books and Vouchers?

You provided an example of attaining improvement by reviewing your books and vouchers. How often must we do it?

Answer

Do it at least once a year. But this is not always easy to remember. So I should like to suggest that you do this to coincide with your inventory-taking which you do at the end of your fiscal year.

On a somewhat related matter, I should like to say something about a survey we made reviewing our system of sending documents. Once I gave a command to a secretariat to review its practice of sending documents on a regular basis to company employees. It sent a questionnaire to those who were on its mailing list with the following words: "We trust that the documents we send to you every week are helpful to you. If you want us to continue sending these documents to you, please so indicate with an X mark." Well, even as a matter of courtesy, the readers would have to place an X mark. Its conclusion was: "Since we have had so many affirmative X signs, we must continue sending these documents without fail to everyone." Not a single copy was dropped from circulation!

My solution to this problem is to rewrite the questionnaire as follows: "To promote efficiency, we have decided to cut the number of documents sent out every week into one-half. We hope to include the documents we are sending to you in this reduction program, and should appreciate your cooperation. If at a future time, you find that these documents are needed, we shall be happy to reactivate your name on our mailing list. But at this time your cooperation would be very much appreciated. If we can count on your cooperation, kindly so indicate by placing an X mark." People are generally very helpful, and with this we can proceed with our efficiency movement.

Question 6. Will a Distortion Arising from Efficiency in One Area Be Forced upon Another Area?

When you promote efficiency in administrative and technology-related divisions, don't you sometimes fear that those areas which require long-range commitment may be sacrificed? For example, the following projects may be terminated: "service to those companies or factories to whom our goods are delivered (our corporate customers)," "assistance to our subcontractors" and "education and nurturing of our human resources."

Answer

The projects which you named, if unattended, do not have an immediate impact on the company. However, from the point of view of having a long-range plan, the company could suffer very severely. Therefore, none of them must be sacrificed in the name of efficiency. Our movement is committed to removing one type of waste after another. I must re-emphasize the fact that it does not plan to eliminate what is needed.

However, I must caution you that those in charge of projects which are important from a long-range perspective do not have a license to continue doing things the same way year in and year out. Their procedures must be continuously improved to respond to changing conditions. If any project is conducted in the same manner as it was three years earlier, then you can be sure that there is waste.

Question 7. If Another Division Tells You Not to Eliminate the Project, How Do You Respond?

You are reviewing to see "if this work can be eliminated," and a request comes from another division: "Don't eliminate it please; we will be inconvenienced." What is one supposed to do?

Answer

If you hear another party saying "Don't eliminate it please; we will be inconvenienced," continue your review process, and respond to this request as follows: "Please let us know which part of our operations you want us to retain. We will do that, but the remainder can still be eliminated." From my experience I know that a cut which would really hurt anyone normally consists of only 10 to 20 percent of the whole.

This is an example from another company. Someone thought that the monthly newsletter was a waste and stopped its distribution. Only two parties complained: "Why haven't we received this month's newsletter?" People were sent to these two parties, asking what type of information they needed. Of the 40-page publication, what they needed was only one-half a page worth of information. Having clarified this matter, the company stopped publication of the monthly newsletter, and continued to send the information requested by the two parties by other means.

In a case like this, if the company said from the outset: "We plan to suspend publication of our monthly newsletter," more likely than not, the response would be "Don't do it please; it's going to inconvenience us." But when we got to the bottom of it, only a very small part of the newsletter was needed.

What is an ideal situation? If those parties consulted by you can say "If you retain only this portion, we do not mind your eliminating the rest," then you have it made!

Question 8. When Will All the Improvement Plans Be on Hand?

Like Toyoda Gosei, my company is also in the midst of conducting an efficiency promotion movement. But there is one difference. We let each of the sections formulate its own schedule for implementing its improvement plan. These plans contain information which management needs, such as "How many man-hours does each of the sections plan to eliminate?", "What is the schedule of its implementation?" and other improvement projects which are noted on a monthly basis from January to December. However, even by March, we still do not have all the improvement plans on hand. On the basis of those plans already submitted, our man-hour reduction project falls short of the target by more than 50 percent. What can we do at this juncture?

Answer

At Toyoda Gosei, too, we do not make a comprehensive list of all the improvement plans at the beginning of the year. We know only the following at that time: those plans which were made near the end of the previous year and were already in the process of being implemented, and those plans which are about to be initiated and whose ideas are known to us. That is all. During the year, we continue our improvement activities by challenging the goals we set for ourselves. As we improve, we look for the next target. Improvement is made over what has already been improved. It is a continuous process and we never let up on it the entire year. Improvement means nothing more and nothing less.

Question 9. What Do You Mean When You Say You Are Making Staff Versatile?

In trying to make your staff more efficient, you need to make them more versatile. Can you enlighten us further on this subject?

Answer

The amount of work the staff has to handle varies greatly from time to time. If staff members are specialists in certain fields and cannot do anything but their specializations, you may experience the following situation: At a certain month, some of them are exceptionally busy, while others remain idle.

If staff members become versatile, they can extend as well as receive help among themselves, thus balancing the situation described above.

Suppose you have 10 members in your staff office, and you have withdrawn two members from there (a 20 percent reduction). The remaining eight must learn to do the work of the two withdrawn by each sharing part of the two's responsibilities. They are exposed to the kind of work they have not done before. Naturally, they do have to study. To be able to respond to changing conditions, and to promote efficiency, versatility is required.

Here is an example from a company which manufactures industrial equipment. They have two divisions, Y and S, divided along the lines of the machines they manufacture. For several years, they have had ups and downs in the orders received. In certain years, the Y division was exceptionally busy, and in others it was the turn of the S division to be busy. The company studied the matter and came up with several plans, one of which called for "making design engineers versatile."

If Y's design engineers are overworked, the relatively free design engineers from S come to their aid. In this case, versatility is of course required. Naturally, the first-rate design engineer of S cannot match skills with the first-rate design engineer of Y and do the same type of work immediately. However, they are only coming to help, so an understanding is reached that the first-rate design engineer from S may do second- or third-rate work at Y. Even when at one division the work is first-rate and at another the work is third-rate, by being versatile the engineers can help the company's overall performance.

Generally speaking, engineers do not want to go to another division and be satisfied with doing a third-rate job there. But at this company, an atmosphere is created to encourage and value "versatility." From what I can see, everyone actively participated in this worthwhile endeavor.

Question 10. What Is the Level of Your Middle Management's Managerial Capabilities?

Mr. Nemoto, I understand that before becoming president of Toyoda Gosei, you gave seminars and lectures on improving managerial capabilities to the middle management of the same company for two years. So when you became president, you already had a middle management with a higher level of managerial capabilities. Your efficiency movement has been a success, which may be due in part to what had been done before. What is your opinion on this?

41

Answer

When I gave those seminars you mentioned, I emphasized this one particular point: "On those matters which fall under your jurisdiction which you consider important, what approaches or solutions do you have of your own?"

As I began the present efficiency promotion movement, each of the division managers and section chiefs had a very clear-cut notion of "What must I do on my own?" This thought process seemed to come naturally. One of the characteristics of the present movement was that "each division maximizes its own special attributes and uses its own ingenuity." Each of these divisions was to create its own method of promotion and implementation. Thus the middle management went about their tasks enthusiastically.

"What can a division manager do on his own?" or "What can a section chief do on his own?" may sound simple but it is not. There are many people to whom functioning independently can never come naturally. So it is necessary to allow time to give these people special training. If managers are not so equipped, we cannot truthfully speak of "each division utilizing its own method."

In QC, we emphasize plan, do, check and action. We must execute the planning phase well in this connection. As for planning, it is not enough just to establish goals. We must at the same time think carefully about the methods of implementing them.

Question 11. How Effective Is the Use of Office Automation Machines in Promoting Efficiency?

In your first point to consider, you mentioned that we must begin with "elimination of waste," which is followed by "office automation (OA)." But you did not explain anything about OA. Can you share your thoughts on this subject with us?

Answer

As I discussed earlier in the text, OA is one of the methods for implementing efficiency. I say that "elimination of waste through the Toyota production system" and "OA" are our two pillars. However, in implementation, I want to say that "OA definitely comes after elimination of waste."

All of our divisions are following this principle and are about to begin preparing and testing for OA. There are so many different types of equipment and machines available for office automation which have developed so rapidly. We must study carefully how they can be most effectively utilized.

3

Policy Control
and Middle Management

It has been more than 20 years since I first began preparing annual policies. I was a division manager when I first drafted an annual policy for my division. I remember being given an opportunity to present a report on the progress of my annual policy when Toyota was examined for the Deming application prize in 1965. Through that encounter, I became convinced that annual policies play a significant role in companies.

In those days, there were some division managers who would say: "Oh, it's that time of the year again to draft the annual policy. I hate it." But I only saw positive advantages and utilized them to the fullest. In planning for something which required six months or one year to implement, superiors and subordinates would have to get together to reach a consensus. Better communication resulted from this. As for implementation, it was made easier, as the time for checking the results was always clearly stated.

As a president today, I am grateful to the institution of annual policy which provides me with opportunities to reach a consensus with my directors while discussing our long-range plans and annual policies.

I. How to Establish Goals

Until about 10 years ago, I used to say that goals must be established through necessity and possibility, and superiors and subordinates must jointly determine their common goals as if they were engaged in catching a ball. However, after the first oil crisis, conditions surrounding management became increasingly difficult, and I now say that goals must be determined through necessity alone. This is so because whatever goals there are which are necessary for management success, they must be attained.

When we think of possibility first, the goal thus established becomes no longer the one with a challenge. Goals are there to challenge people, and cannot be regarded merely as previews of things yet to come.

With regards to the rate of defectives and rate of accidents, I ask my subordinates to set their goals as high as any in their own categories. If another workplace accomplishes that much, we must aspire to do likewise, and that is the message I wish to convey. There is no point in setting our sight on the second best. This does not mean that setting an intermediate goal is wrong. For example, if we are at the C level, we can aspire to reach the B level within a year, and then move on to meet the challenge of level A.

In establishing a goal, there is another factor which must be carefully considered. That is the persuasiveness of the targeted value.

For example, to "set your sight at the best in your category" described above, is persuasive. Even if the target is quite far off from present conditions, it incites the workers to want to meet the challenge.

Now let us consider a goal set to reduce cost. For the purpose of obtaining a profit, a reduction of 1.5 billion yen would be sufficient. But the company decided to set 2 billion yen as the target. Assuming that the figure of 1.5 billion yen would be persuasive, but 2 billion yen would not, then this goal would be a failure.

The goal is not necessarily better when it is bigger. If it is bigger and is still persuasive, that is the best. But if a bigger goal lacks persuasiveness, it becomes a failure.

Incidentally, when there is little persuasiveness, the ability to implement correspondingly suffers.

II. Too Many Items in the Divisional Policy—Learn to Stress Only the Priority Items

Divisional policies often have too many items. There is a need to include all the goals contained in the company policy, to which items peculiar to the division are added. Naturally the number of items increases. This tendency is magnified when it reaches the level of sectional policies. Section chiefs naturally want to include everything that their division managers expect of them in their own sectional policies. The upshot is that no one knows what to emphasize when reading these divisional or sectional policies.

In QC we stress the importance of concentrating on a few priority items. This holds true for the subject under discussion. At each level of position he holds, a responsible employee must learn to identify the most important issues for the year, and place emphasis on a few projects which must be implemented within six months to a year.

A divisional policy contains items which the division manager considers important. If asked, he must be able to recite these items. If he has to consult a document before he can state them, it means that he has too many items in his policy. This practice is not to be tolerated.

Generally when a division manager includes too many items in his annual policy, chances are he has not given much thought to the following issues.

1. If the matter is not a priority item for the division as a whole, but is important only to a specific section, that matter need not be included in the division's annual policy. It can be given in the form of an instruction to the specific section chief. For example, instructions to security and power divisions of a plant need not be included in the plant manager's annual policy.

2. One's own division may be designated to assist in the implementation of priority items of other divisions. In such a case, there is no need to recite every item of cooperative endeavor in one's own annual policy. The manager can say to the division manager who is responsible for those items: "As soon as you establish a concrete plan, you can count on our cooperation." That can take care of this issue.

3. There are people who feel that what was good for the past year is good enough for the coming year. So they deem it unnecessary to establish any new goals. Yet if nothing is written on the annual policy, there may be suspicion that they are not doing anything. So they include items simply for the sake of including them.

For example, a division which has been the top-rated one in re-

47

ducing the number of equipment failures need not repeat it in its annual policy. When a certain item does not appear in the annual policy, it does not mean that the division has abandoned the task. It simply means that it will continue to do as much as it has done in the past.

When a certain item appears in the annual policy, it means that the division is going to place a special emphasis on that project. It usually includes things which have not been adequately done in the past. Thus, if "shortening the lead time" appears as an item in the annual policy, everyone knows what the division plans to do in the coming year.

III. What Must the Division Manager and Section Chief Do?

The following discussion applies both to the divisional policy and the sectional policy. Assuming that 10 items are included in the policy, does this mean that the division manager (or section chief) himself must determine concrete implementation plans for all 10 items? The answer is in the negative.

Now, as a general theory, I shall divide these items into three categories for more explanation.

Of the 10, the division manager must be the initiator of ideas for two or three items and provide concrete implementation plans for them. These are important items for which the subordinates do not seem to be able to supply good ideas, hence the necessity for the division manager's direct action.

For the next two or three items, the division manager does not have to establish implementation plans. His main contribution is to provide "points to consider." As for concrete steps, let the subordinates initiate them.

For the remainder, simply provide the goals, and then let the subordinates use their initiative in formulating concrete implementation plans. Volunteer some advice when asked. But do not give directions from A to Z. It will spoil the subordinates' willingness to participate.

The above are common sense suggestions. But in the real world common sense is often not practiced. There are many people who do not know the meaning of "the division manager must devise his own methods." There are some who feel that the function of a division manager is merely to say "Do your best, do your best." That is not work, is it?

In this difficult day and age, there are always problems which require the division manager to present his own ideas and establish implementation plans. That is why we have division managers in the first place. The same applies to all section chiefs.

Let me cite an example. I visited a company with about 500 employees. While making the rounds of its factory, I asked a section chief: "Can you tell me the most important problem you have to solve this year?"

"I have 60 subordinates," the section chief responded. "This year we want to implement the Toyota production system thoroughly, and reduce man-hours by 10 percent (which is translated into a reduction of six workers). We began this project in January and since then six months have passed. I shall now discuss its progress."

He explained that there were six subsections in his section, labeled A through F. Each of the subsections consisted of 10 workers, including its subsection foreman. Subsection A changed the placement of equipment and machines, improved distribution of workload and succeeded in reducing one worker. Similarly, subsection B was able to withdraw one worker. Subsection C also withdrew a worker, but since its machines fail occasionally, it was common to have two-hour overtime daily. The section chief concluded his remarks by saying that he wanted to take measures to eliminate equipment failure, and "eliminate the two-hour overtime."

"Mr. Section Chief," I asked, "is that the only problem you have to worry about? Is there anything else?" Was the elimination of overtime really a problem for the section chief? Should not the issue of equipment failure be left to subsection foreman C to solve? I felt that the section chief had no clear-cut notion of how to reduce three more workers in the six months remaining to him.

"Can you withdraw one worker each from subsections D, E and F?" was my next question. "The foremen of D, E and F do not seem to understand the Toyota production system as well as the foremen of A, B, and C," I continued. "Therefore I do not think you will be able to reach your goal by the end of this year. Doesn't that worry you?" "Exactly," was his response, confirming my suspicion.

The task before this section chief was to make his workers thoroughly understand the Toyota production system. His annual policy contained this item, but after six months, he still had not found the right method to implement it. He could let the foreman of C worry about the equipment failure. His task was what to do with D, E and F.

If I were the section chief, I would have placed my emphasis on thoroughly educating the three subsections in the Toyota production

49

system. I would pay special attention to enhancing the ability of the three subsection foremen in undertaking improvement projects.

I would establish a model line in subsection D, and once a week during the months of June and July I would personally instruct them. I would ask foremen from E and F to attend, and the foreman from A would be asked to serve as my assistant. In August and September, I would go to subsection E, and in October and November I would go to subsection F. They would take turns, learning more about the Toyota production system.

If we were lucky, each of the subsections would succeed in reducing its work force by one person. But even if some of them would not succeed before year-end, we could look forward to the coming year. Not only that, with the improved ability of the three foremen, many good things could be expected of them.

Nothing can be accomplished by giving a stern command to these foremen, saying "complete these tasks before year-end." It might work for those foremen who know the Toyota production system. But for those who do not know it, the command would be useless. The task of the section chief is to provide appropriate guidance. If he, himself, is not equipped to give such guidance, he can establish an educational plan and retain the services of outside instructors.

This is what I mean by the task which must be performed by the section chief.

IV. Middle Management's Items for Implementation

As described in the above example, the items of implementation for middle management generally consist of "soft" items. While the foreman handles the "hard" items (e. g., reducing the incidence of machine failure), the section chief is engaged in a "soft" item, implementing training in the Toyota production system. Let us call this "implementation of special training."

In addition, "considering the introduction of a new method of QC promotion," comes under the category of "soft" items. This may involve establishment of a committee to promote efficiency in connection with the efficiency movement of administrative divisions, or setting up QC circle leadership meetings once a month to support QC circle activities.

Another example is that of "organizing a team." When things do not move smoothly under the present organizational setup, an ad hoc team may be organized.

There are actually many types of teams. There can be a team which is responsible for drafting improvement plans, and there can be a team which is responsible for testing and confirming the test results.

There are three things to consider in making team activities a success. They are:

1. Team members must be named by their immediate superior. The QC secretariat may feel that its responsibility is to name team members. But the secretariat is merely an outsider, and team members named by it may not always find it easy to attend meetings. If team members are named by their section chief, this problem does not arise.

2. Select a veteran worker to head the team. Choose the most senior man who is also endowed with leadership ability and the ability to grasp all major issues.

3. Set a firm deadline. As soon as the team's activities are begun, establish the dates of its interim report and final report. The team consists of members from different divisions. If there is no established deadline, its work may drag on. When the team makes a report, be sure to have the superiors of its constituent members present.

Next in the implementation items is that of "concentrating on priorities." As discussed earlier, there are so many things one wishes to do, but time does not allow it. It is necessary to establish an order of priority, showing which item must be handled first, and which item must be emphasized. For example, there is a theme calling for cost reduction. The following question must be immediately answered: "Which comes first, the cost of materials, the cost of processing or the cost of purchasing from subcontractors?" It is the responsibility of the section chief to determine the order of priority.

"New points to consider," may come as the next item. For example, in the efficiency promotion movement for the administrative divisions, a view is presented to apply "the approach of the Toyota production system in office procedures." That will constitute a new point of view. Another may come from the thought that "we do not withdraw people from the work force after the improvement. Let us withdraw workers first and then start our improvement activities." These new points of view may be determined by the superiors and then handed down, or ideas may be first given by them and discussed by all before a decision is made. In any event, new points of view are born.

Another fairly common implementation item can be found in "holding study groups and presentation meetings." This can be considered part of the "implementation of special training" discussed earlier. Here are a number of examples.

The chief of a section consisting of 20 staff members who are specialists in their own fields heard this comment: "It's difficult to understand what your people are saying. I think they are too specialized."

Thereupon the section chief decided to establish a policy that "within a year, the entire staff of 20 people will endeavor to speak in a way that others can understand." He was motivated by the fact that his section performed staff functions for the entire company, and one of its important responsibilities was to go to other divisions to explain or persuade them on technical and other matters. He could not treat the remarks he heard lightly.

Normally, a section chief may simply say: "Hey guys, people are saying that they can't understand what you are saying. Change your way of presentation, will you," and then dismiss the matter. But not this section chief. He felt it was necessary to create a special device that would make this project a success. He organized internal presentation meetings, held monthly, the purpose of which was to make the speeches easily understood by nonspecialists. Each of the staff members made two presentations a year.

The section chief had a nonspecialist attend these meetings as a monitor. If this nonspecialist could understand the talk, he would give it a pass mark, and if he could not understand the talk, he would give it a failure mark. After a year, almost everyone was able to get a pass mark. This method of implementation proved to be exceptionally effective.

This unique idea of having a monitor present at the meetings could be proposed only by the section chief. His subordinates could not be expected to come up with the same idea. This is the reason why I consider the above to be one of the best examples of the initiatives taken by section chiefs in handling their "implementation items."

Interim Inspection and the Interim Report

I instituted the practice of "making an interim inspection after six months have elapsed and reporting on it" a mandatory part of a division manager's annual policy. At first, some division managers balked and would say: "It's only half a year since we started, and we spent the first three months in preparation. The project has just begun, and I have very little to report. Can I pass?"

I am not asking them to provide me with the final results. I want to know what methods and implementation items they have devised, and how far they have gone with them. If they proceed at the present pace, can they reach their goals by the end of the year? These are matters which are of concern to me.

Managers who make the interim check will benefit from the practice. If problems are found, they can be corrected. The president likes to know if his managers are on the ball with regard to these "interim actions." There are instances in which he may come to the managers' aid, and he may want to devise action plans of his own.

Let me present another story which is related to this subject. That is "checking conditions at the takeoff stage." The "interim checking," referred to above, is usually undertaken after six months, but the "takeoff" normally refers to the first three months after the beginning of the plan. In implementing an annual policy, one is especially anxious to know if those important new plans have taken off smoothly. Therefore we must engage in "checking conditions at the takeoff stage." In checking, we can ask questions such as: "Are all systems operating smoothly within the division to promote efficiency?" or "Have we completed our first survey for shortening the lead time?" The word "takeoff" (*suberidashi*) gives an uplifting and at the same time smooth, flowing feeling, and it is a popular phrase among workers.

Inept Administrators

Who are excellent administrators and who are inept administrators?

"As far as improvement is concerned, that's your job. I will be happy to gather and summarize your reports for our superior." Someone who speaks in this fashion is an inept administrator. In promoting efficiency, there are many problems which require the personal attention of middle management. When coordination with another division is required, or when a difficult technical problem arises, the staff and superiors must be consulted. It is the responsibility of the administrator to perform these tasks and not that of his subordinates. If problems are complicated, it may even be necessary to organize several teams along the lines of the problem themes they have to solve. But again organizing such teams is the responsibility of the administrator.

Conversely, there may be some administrators who insist: "I decide how to do this job. Leave all the thinking to me." This is also proof positive of an inept administrator. In administrative divisions, no superior can know everything about the work performed by his workers. In fact, some managers even do not know how to write a voucher. Improvement for these types of work must be conducted with full participation of respective individual workers. Let them think about improvement and accept their suggestions.

An excellent administrator is one who tackles improvement problems on his own, and at the same time allows each and every one of his subordinates to participate in the improvement projects.

V. Questions and Answers

Question 1. How Do You Interface Technology Development with the Company's Annual Policy?

Our company's annual policy contains annual goals for quality and cost which are interfaced with the methods to attain them. However, when we speak of technology development and new market development, we cannot know the results until three or five years later. Their implementation plans cannot be properly interfaced with our annual policy goals. How can we handle this problem?

Answer

Themes such as "reduction in delivery of defective quality goods" relative to quality, and "reaching value engineering goals" relative to costs can be interfaced exactly with the annual goals and implementation items. However, methods and implementation items of technology development and new market development do not interface with the annual goals. The only conceivable connection they have is with the company's long-range policy goals. For example, an item may be inserted in the long-range policy stating that "sales and profits both are to be raised by 50 percent five years from now." To reach that goal, a policy of technology development is initiated which is incorporated as part of the company's five-year plan.

To answer your question, transcribe the first-year implementation plan of the long-range policy on the columns for methods and implementation in your annual policy. If there is a column for the fiscal year, leave it blank. If it will make you feel better having something written in that column, enter the goals of the long-range policy there, but for reference purposes only, and your entry must be bracketed to differentiate it from other regular entries.

I have just said to "transcribe." You actually have a choice of briefly transcribing the methods for the first-year period of a long-range plan, or writing more concretely about the goals. If you choose the latter, you may enter not only information concerning the first year, but also that of the second year. Some items are carried over from one year to another, and this practice makes perfectly good sense. When you want your company to make all systems ready for a new development project, it is wise to provide specific information in the annual policy to secure cooperation across the board.

Question 2. What Is the Relationship Between Human Resource Development and Annual Policy Goals?

In listening to your talk, it becomes clear that on the matter of human resource development, we can take steps similar to those taken in technology development. However, in the case of human resource development, it takes longer than five years. If we are to have a longer-range plan like this, what is the most appropriate way of handling it?

Answer

In nurturing future key personnel through a long-range system of rotation, the company is making preparation for itself 10 to 20 years hence. There is no exact correlation between this and the company's concrete present goals. There is no need to coordinate this ultra long-range plan with the methods of policy control currently employed.

However, in human resource development, some short-term training programs can be coordinated with annual policy goals. For example, a special training program in the Toyota production system for a group of squad leaders is perfectly consistent with one of the annual goals which calls for reducing man-hours by 15 percent.

Labor relations constitute another area in which interfacing of the goal with method presents difficulties. For example, we may write in our annual policy goals that we shall attempt to "deepen the sense of trust between management and labor." The phrase itself does not indicate in any way how the relations between the two parties progressed in the past year, or how things may develop in the coming year based on what happened in the past. It merely reaffirms the basic position which the company takes, that it wishes to abide by a sense of mutual trust. From the point of view of "setting priorities," discussed earlier, labor relations need not be included in the annual policy. But an exception must be made in this case, because it reaffirms the basic stands which the company takes in managing its affairs.

Question 3. What Can You Do to Avoid Merely Going Through the Motions of Engaging in Maintenance Control Activities?

In factories, it is extremely important to have good maintenance control activities. Yet if we continue what we did last year in the current fiscal year, will we not be merely going through the motions of following timeworn activities? What can we do to avoid this?

Answer

First I suggest that you take stock of what you did last year. Examine your work situation and determine if you were able to obtain desired results on the matters you emphasized. Ascertain also whether you were able to do things the way you wanted them done.

Assume that last year you provided training to your supervisors on "intermittent checking and how to observe its implementation." In factories, you check your products intermittently; that is, once every hour, or one out of every 100 pieces. But often this system of intermittent checking was not followed closely according to standards set, and your supervisors would overlook it. Your training was directed to this very issue, and it was a success, as no incidence of overlooking was reported.

However, a new problem arises. When a defective piece is discovered through the intermittent checking, how do you deal with those pieces which are produced before and after the piece in question? How many of them must be checked? You have committed a number of errors in this regard. Now the answer is obvious. For this year, you can establish a new target; that is, to train your supervisors in the methods of investigating and identifying pieces when an abnormality occurs.

In this case, the rationale is that your own workplace is still not up to par, and this requires personnel training to be used as a lever in raising the consciousness level of the workers about maintenance control activities. If no new problems arise in your own workplace, you can use the problems existing in similar workplaces as text materials for training. In any event, it is good to change your approach so those who are receiving the training can be exposed to something new, and therefore not become stale in their knowledge.

Question 4. What Are the Goals for Implementation Items?

In order to reach our goals, we create and utilize implementation items. Now you say that we must establish goals for the implementation items. That is quite confusing. Can you elaborate on this further?

Answer

Have you ever heard a report like this at a year-end audit for policy goals? "The goal established for this year's man-hour reduction was 15 percent. In order to reach this goal, we felt it was necessary to raise the aptitude of the squad leader class to facilitate improvement. Thus as our implementation item, we instituted a special training program in the Toyota production system for the squad leader class. The training proceeded smoothly according to schedule, and we are happy to report that we have reached the goal of a 15 percent reduction in man-hours."

There is something missing in this report. It does not indicate that "the aptitude for improvement" has been enhanced. If the decision to provide training was reached rather lightly when the matter was first discussed, then it would not be possible to report later that "the aptitude for improvement increased by this much." This is so because they initially decided on their implementation items without giving much thought to them. If the level of the squad leader class was low, that fact should have been duly noted and the target for improvement within a year clearly shown.

For example, at present with regard to the aptitude for improvement, only 20 percent of the squad leader class is in the A category, 50 percent in the B category and the remaining 30 percent in the C category. A goal can be set of having 50 percent in the A category and 50 percent in the B category by the end of the year. If the implementation plan is carried out in this fashion, at the end of the year they can report that "the level has been raised by this much." This is what I call the goal for an implementation item.

Let me add another example to make the point perfectly clear. At one assembly plant, a new assembly line was established to manufacture a new model car. At this line, the ratio of experienced workers was about one-half of other normal lines. To make certain that it could engage in the mass production of these new cars without a hitch, it was decided to increase the number of processes where hand-held small tools are replaced by simple automated devices. In conceiving your plan, do not use the word "more," but state your goal as follows: "We shall have 200 or more items of simple automated devices instead of 100 items or so as in the past."

If goals are set for implementation items in this fashion, more care will be taken in establishing the implementation items. When clear-cut goals are given, workers will show great willingness to reach them.

Things are not always as difficult as they appear when establishing goals for implementation items. For example: "Policy goal: Reducing the term of work in manufacturing of metal molds by 30 days. First implementation item: Reducing the design period by 10 days" may look a bit complicated. But a 10 day reduction in the design period is derived naturally by dividing the overall goal into its logical components. In this case, do not think too hard. Do what is normally done, and you can meet most of the requirements discussed here.

Question 5. What Are the Implementation Items for Staff Divisions?

Divisions such as the division of quality assurance and the division of health and safety serve a staff function for the entire company. Their main responsibilities are to establish goals and implementation items for the company and to make adjustments and check the progress of these goals and items. They also have implementation items and goals which are peculiar to their own divisions. When they establish their own divisions' policy statements, they may confuse functions peculiar to their own with the companywide ones. How can we prevent this from happening?

Answer

When policy statements are drafted, the two functions must be written separately. The goals and implementation items which are determined when they act in the staff capacity must be identified as "company policy." Within these company policies, there are some items which must be handled by these staff divisions. They then become "divisional policies." If company policy and divisional policies are to be listed on a single sheet of paper, draw a line between the two to differentiate them.

Question 6. How Do We Reexamine and Review Implementation Items?

When we determine the coming year's policy, we review the degree of its implementation in the present year. At that point, we check the actual accomplishments against the goals established. But often we do our reviewing pro forma. How can we make our reviewing process better?

Answer

There are people who will say: "As long as we reach our goals, it does not matter a whiff about the implementation items." This way of thinking is not suitable in conducting a successful TQC program. Those were the same implementation items which were determined at the beginning of the year after all issues were carefully studied. If they were not well implemented, and yet the goals were reached, then something went wrong when these implementation items were determined. Conversely, if goals were not reached in spite of the fact that the implementation items were carefully followed, other implementation items should have been adopted in the first place. A review made at this juncture gives us an opportunity to restudy the manner in which we have been determining our implementation items.

The method of promotion must also come under scrutiny. Ask yourselves these questions: "Have we been able to promote the implementation items and schedule things in the way we wanted?" and "Have we engaged in interim checking and taken corrective actions?" All of these self-checks are designed to make sure that similar mistakes will never occur again.

Question 7. How Does One Make Sure That Remaining Problems and Future Development Are Not Made Obscure?

At the year-end inspection, we ask our subordinates to write about remaining problems and the method of continuing our work in the future. Often their writings are hazy and not up to par. How can we improve this?

Answer

I face a similar problem rather frequently, but my advice to my subordinates is simple: "It does not have to be elaborate, just give me some of the concrete ideas you have." I ask them to submit their general outline with a rough schedule. For example, "We plan to form a team by early February," or "I plan to set up individualized training sessions by the first of March."

Once in a while I encounter people like this: "I just finished completing work on some remaining problems. Please do not ask me to think about future plans." What a pity! He is denying himself a good opportunity. A week ago he completed his report with supporting documents appended to it. The report dealt with a remaining problem which was important to him. In the process of writing his report, and in rethinking it through after its completion, he should by now have some ideas on what to do next. If he chooses to present his ideas about the future, he could append a note to his completed report and make some additional comments orally. It is not a difficult task, and the opportunity must not be missed.

Question 8. What Do You Think of Providing Explanations for Divisional Policies?

When we write our annual policy statements, they often include the following phrases: "We are going to facilitate that. . . ." or "We are going to fulfill this aspect. . . ." In order to make certain that everyone understands them, we want to write explanations to these policies and publish them in the form of a booklet. How do you react to this idea?

Answer

If you meet with your subordinates on a one-to-one basis when issuing your annual policies and implementation items, explanation is seldom necessary. If you institute a new policy which states that "Local restriction on noise pollution is going to be very strict starting January, so an anti-noise pollution team must be expeditiously formed," you do not need a booklet of explanation. However, if you are going to ask your subordinates to help you implement a policy of "making a comprehensive system of handling cost planning," you need a booklet. You must show them why you are establishing this policy, by what date you expect it to be completed and at what level you want the system to have an impact.

For policies like the one just described, explanation booklets are a must. Generally, if a policy is based on a long-range consideration, or if you have more than one goal, it is best to provide explanation booklets.

Be sure to explain to your subordinates why you have chosen this theme, what is expected of them and how to focus attention on specific issues. If all of these issues must be included in the text of your policy statement, it becomes too long and obscures the main points. Yes, in special cases such as this, you are right in wanting to have explanation booklets.

Question 9. What Are the Implementation Items Which Cannot Be Included in Your Annual Policy?

No matter how important the issue may be, there are certain things which must not be put into writing by a company or a division in its annual policy. How shall we treat these issues?

Answer

Here are some examples of those matters which cannot be included in the annual policy statement. They are: personnel change, change in the organizational structure, mergers, increase of capital and purchase of land. These may be some of the most important issues the company must implement in the coming year, but they must be kept secret except from a select few. Therefore, they cannot be published in the annual policy statement. Seen from another perspective, the annual policy statement is issued to obtain cooperation for established policies on a companywide basis. The matters cited above can always be implemented by only a few people, so there is no need to publish them.

4

Motivating
Employee Participation in
Improvement Activities

As described in "my credo" contained in Chapter 1, I believe in "improvement after improvement"—and it represents my way of life.

You are managers and supervisors who are committed to creating workplaces that show a desire to improve. In this chapter, may I share with you my 30 years of experience which has also been devoted to improvement? May I present the lessons I have learned in the form of the "attitude" managers must foster in dealing with employees under them?

Principle I. The Superior Must Also Engage in Improvement

There are some managers who feel that improvement activities are for their subordinates but not for themselves. If a manager or a supervisor wants to encourage strong employee participation in improvement activities, he must be prepared to undertake the task himself first. Unless he does so, his subordinates will not listen to him.

This is a story from my Toyota Motors days. The president of a certain machine tool company came to see me with one of his plant managers.

"A year ago, we initiated our suggestion system," said the president. "We received your forms and regulations, changed the name of the company to that of ours, but retained everything else exactly the way you had when we started our program. It has been a year now, but seldom do we receive suggestions from our employees. What kind of change must we make, so we may receive as many suggestions as Toyota receives?"

I responded with a question: "Mr. President, how often do you use the word 'improvement' in a month?"

There was no answer from the other end, so I turned my question to the plant manager: "How about you, Mr. Manager?"

All they could say was that they might have uttered the word once or twice in a month. There was probably no flaw in the organization of the suggestion system, but it would not have a chance to succeed as long as this attitude persisted.

Suggestions are born when people look at their own work and start asking themselves: "Is there a better way of doing this?" Unless there is a sense of discovering problems constantly, no suggestion can emerge.

Unless a superior constantly mentions "improvement after improvement," and means what he says, his subordinates will have no incentive to consider improvement. Actually this is not all. The superior must also be determined to engage in improvement activities on his own to set a good example.

When I was a plant manager, I engaged in improvement activities day and night, and I constantly preached the virtue of "improvement after improvement." I did this, in part, to encourage employee participation in improvement activities.

Presidents and plant managers may adopt different themes for improvement from the themes adopted by line workers. Line workers are more interested in what they actually see and do, and may adopt as their themes such slogans as "order of work" or "tools." Presidents and plant managers are more likely to select "soft" improvement themes, such as "structure," "organization" and "office procedures."

While the fields they choose may differ in concrete terms, as long as those who are above continue to speak of and practice "improvement after improvement," those who are below will also become imbued with the notion of improvement. This is one of the keys in making a suggestion system work.

There is another issue which I wish to raise with managers and supervisors. That is "the attitude of the superior toward improvement." If management does not have a good attitude, no matter how good a system may be, success will become elusive.

Let us now turn to the issue of attitude.

Principle II. Show an Interest in the Subordinates' Improvement Activities

There are still far too many managers who feel that their work consists of giving their subordinates a set of goals and nothing more. "You must engage in this many improvement activities" and "You must engage in so many hours of activities," are examples of orders issued in this fashion. After giving perfunctory words of encouragement, these managers may sit back and wait until statistics are compiled. How can they expect to have their subordinates show any interest in improvement activities?

To avoid this pitfall, may I suggest that superiors always show an interest in what their subordinates are doing. "What kind of improvement have you been able to bring to your workplace?" "What are you planning now?" These are some of the questions they can ask of their subordinates.

A while back, I visited S Motors and heard this example of improvement by a female worker in its general affairs section.

One of the responsibilities of the general affairs section is to receive and distribute the day's mail. One day the girl discovered that a special delivery letter and a regular letter, both sent from the same place and on the same date, arrived in the office at the same time. She came to her subsection chief and suggested: "I suspect that letters sent from this end are treated in the same manner. May I use prepaid reply cards to check this out?" The subsection chief immediately gave his assent, saying "Good, I am glad you noticed that. Go ahead." The result confirmed her suspicion. For letters sent to nearby cities and prefectures, there was no difference in special delivery and regular mail. Delivery to the business establishments was so frequent that regular mail reached its destination as early as special delivery letters. The company immediately changed its practice, using only regular mail. Just with this one single modification, a substantial sum was saved.

There are two important points to this story. The first is that the girl has always been working with the thought of finding something which requires improvement. If she had been working with an attitude that improvement is none of her concern, she would not have been able to notice this when it occurred. Or even when she noticed it, she might not have been interested in pursuing it any further.

Another important point is the attitude of the subsection chief. For our purpose, this is even more important than the attitude of the female worker.

It was good that when she first noticed it, he immediately responded: "Good, I am glad you noticed that. Go ahead." Suppose he had said instead: "The money we spend in special delivery is a pittance. Forget about it. Now bring me a cup of tea." He would have poured cold water on the desire for improvement.

Fortunately, this subsection chief has always had an interest in his subordinates' improvement activities. So on that particular day, he could say very naturally, "Good show!" or "I am glad you noticed that."

In a similar vein, I urge superiors to listen carefully to what their subordinates say in QC circle meetings. They are making important presentations. If their superior shows no interest, a letdown feeling can become pervasive. It will be difficult for them to become motivated for the next improvement project.

I give the following advice to companies which promote QC circle activities.

It costs time and money to hold a companywide meeting, and we cannot have too many of them. As an alternative, you may want to organize a number of small-scale meetings to give circles a chance to make presentations, an opportunity otherwise denied them in the companywide meeting. The small-scale meetings can be organized by division or section. If you want to simplify the process further, you can adopt a system of "circuit hearings." I have used this device along with other methods since the time I was a plant manager. I have used "circuit hearings" not only to listen to reports of QC circles but also those of foremen.

Reproduced below are contents of these "circuit hearings." It is a mini-mini edition of our regular improvement idea presentation meetings.

1. Persons involved—foremen and QC circle leaders.
2. Contents of presentation—examples of improvement.
3. Time—three minutes.
4. Documentation or supporting materials—a full poster-size sheet (103 × 145.6 cm, or 40.6 × 57.6 inches) plus the actual item.
5. Form of written report—include in the report only points to be emphasized in the improvement activity. (The reasons for choosing this theme and other matters may be presented orally.)

The difference between these series of hearings and normal presentation meetings is that in the former, I go to the workplace and hear their reports directly. They can show the actual items on which improvement has been made. It creates an environment which makes things easier and more fun for the person who is making the report, and that sentiment is shared by the listener also.

Another difference is that in this instance, the time is limited to three minutes. Some say this is too short, but if you have the actual item in front of you, three minutes is all that is needed to know most of the issues connected to the theme. Of course, you can expand each of these presentations into a 15-minute session, and the degree of understanding will be further enhanced. But it means that there will be fewer people who will be allowed to participate. I want to hear from as many people as possible, hence the creation of the three-minute format. In this way, I can wander around a workplace for two hours and listen to reports from more than 20 persons.

Principle III. Never Say: "What? Are You Doing That Kind of Improvement Now?"

I want to share with you an example from a division which I used to head. As part of the division's annual policy, I established a goal of "improvement of office procedures." The improvement activities were to be carried out through suggestions made by everyone in the division. In May, I was to meet with each person individually to hear from him about an example of his own improvement activities.

One day in May, a female worker came to my office. She was selected by lot to make her presentation that day. Here is her story.

"My work begins at 8:30. First I go to the Technology Section and receive a box full of vouchers and chits, return to my own section and then deliver these documents to workers in two subsections according to their work. It takes 30 minutes to complete my delivery. There is another girl in the next section who does the same work but handles it flawlessly. I wondered how this was possible and investigated it. She has been receiving her documents presorted at the Technology Section. There were several boxes for the other section to which documents were deposited in accordance with separate functions performed by different subsections. I asked: 'Why is it that my section must receive all the documents in one box?' The answer was, 'It has always been that way.' From the next day on, I asked that documents addressed to the people in my section also be presorted. Now I can do my work as well as the girl in the next section. What used to take 30 minutes now takes only 15 minutes."

I was so pleased with this presentation that I convened a general meeting after lunch and gave the following talk:

"I heard a very good example of improvement activity today. Without spending a penny, a fellow worker has increased her efficiency by 15 minutes each day. That is an outstanding improvement. When they hear this, some people may say: 'Don't get smart, buddy. Where have you been all these years, taking you this long to figure it out? By the way, where have your subsection chief and section chief been?' The fact of the matter is no one knew anything about it until our fellow worker discovered it. We have to be grateful to her for that. That is why I caution managers to Never say: 'What? Are you doing that kind of improvement now?' "

I did not discover this until later, but it confirmed my view that the female worker's subsection chief and section chief were good administrators. The subsection chief asked the girl when she drew the lot: "What are you going to say to Mr. Nemoto?" The girl answered: "About the box." She had presented her experience within the subsection, so the chief already knew the story. "That's good," he said. The section chief was also there and added: "Oh, about the box—very good. Mr. Nemoto will be so delighted."

The fact that both the section chief and the subsection chief could anticipate my reaction was commendable. In fact I was so happy that I had to assemble everyone to hear the story!

How about your own experience? Have you ever said to one of your subordinates: "What? Are you doing that kind of improvement now?" I suspect that at least one-third of the readers of this volume has had an experience of that sort, demeaning the efforts of others.

This is actually a very important issue. Please think for a moment, and put yourself on the receiving end. You have done your best for the sake of the company and gave a good report on your improvement activities. You thought you were to be commended, but instead you received sly, demeaning remarks. Taking this one step further, you might have even felt that you were scolded for not discovering the cause of your past inefficiency sooner. If so, what is the use of expending your energy on improvement activities?

The same thing can happen with improvement activities undertaken by middle management also. If their superiors say to them, "What? Are you doing that kind of improvement now?" the point would be lost entirely. That is a phrase which should never be uttered.

Principle IV. Seeds for Improvement Are Limitless

This also happened when I was a plant manager. I was wandering around the plant when a foreman stopped me. "Mr. Nemoto, please listen to what I want to say about my improvement plan."

"Well, I heard from you about it last week," I answered. But his response was: "I improved on what you heard last week. After observing the conditions existing after the improvement, another idea came to me. Can you give me a moment of your time now?"

This is the very essence of improvement. Even if you have made improvement on a problem once, you can always come up with more progressive ideas once you observe the results. In some instances, improvement may be carried out simultaneously over two separate processes.

I am firmly convinced that the seeds for improvement are limitless. I base this statement on the following two factors.

The first is that man's ability is continuously improving.

By improving one aspect, man's ability for improvement is further enhanced. By listening to examples of other people's improvement, one's own ability increases. By studying about equipment, tools and materials to obtain new knowledge, a person's ability again improves. His ability has improved so much that when he restudies what he did six months earlier, he would want to make some improvement on it again.

The second factor is that conditions are constantly changing.

In general terms, conditions surrounding companies are changing. Since the time of the first energy crisis, many improvement plans were proposed from the standpoint of energy saving. In fact, the oil crisis became the catalyst for change. There are also changes in conditions which are peculiar to a manufacturing process. For example, at one process the amount of production is reduced by one-half. If it continues to produce in the same way as before, nothing can go right. The way of thinking must be adjusted for change and new ways devised. In other words, these changes are sowing the seeds for improvement.

These are the types of experiences known to all processes, large and small. That is the reason why I firmly believe that the seeds for improvement are limitless.

Principle V. Have Ears to Listen to the Mistakes
Committed by Subordinates

"Mr. Nemoto, you ask us to give a talk on recent improvement activities," someone said to me, "but we just don't have enough seeds for improvement."

In principle IV, I mentioned that the seeds for improvement are limitless. Even when we do not have a failure, we can still find some seeds for improvement. But when we have a failure, the failure itself becomes a seed for improvement. Those people who say that there is no seed to be found must look around to see if there are no failures or misses. The seeds they can find will indeed be limitless.

Every failure produces an improvement plan for prevention of recurrence. When I fail in something, I may say to myself, "Gosh, I made a mistake." But at the same time I am glad that "I found a seed for improvement." If you can train yourself into thinking this way, you can accomplish a lot.

When someone who works for me makes a mistake, I always say to him: "We are not gods, so we make mistakes. An important thing to remember is that we do not make the same mistake twice. So do your best to prevent recurrence." Normally those employees, managers and line workers alike, who have experienced this would not only help improve the process where the mistake had occurred but also assist other processes in promoting improvement activities.

Quite a while back, I asked the president of a company where I was visiting: "Mr. President, how many times in a month do you hear from your employees about their mistakes and failures?" The answer was that "There was not a single case this month, last month or two months earlier."

I commented: "Isn't it strange that a company with 1,000 workers in its factory does not produce a single mistake in a month which requires the president's attention. My guess is that you have a number of incidents. But if a report is made to the president, those who are responsible will fear being scolded or losing out in the next round of promotion. That is why they no longer report to you."

If the president is prone to anger, and employees do not dare report to him for fear of being scolded, then that is a serious issue for the company. When I was a plant manager, whenever a division manager or section chief came to me to say that he made a mistake, I would immediately say to him: "Please take a seat, and have a cup of tea with me." Through this little show of kindness, I wanted my subordinates to know that I was always ready to listen to their tales of committing mistakes. It is not easy to report to a superior about one's own mistake, and yet he still comes. He is a special person in my book.

I talked to this president about my own ideas, and suggested to him that he might wish to adopt a similar approach. At first, it was not easy to use this method, but once he got used to it, it became second nature to him.

In this chapter, in using the word "to listen," I deliberately used two different characters. One represents the notion of listening rather passively, and the other represents the notion of listening very intently. In the case of listening to mistakes and failures, I uniformly used the latter; that is, "to incline one's own ears to listen with full attention." This is the way I want it to be when my subordinates are good enough to come to share their experiences with me.

Questions and Answers

Question 1. What Is the Difference Between Improvement Activities by Foremen and the Same Activities by QC Circles?

Mr. Nemoto, you said that you wander around to listen to foremen and QC circles about their improvement activities. Generally people do not differentiate between the two. Why is this?

Answer

In the past, foremen took charge of QC circle activities, and the two activities could not be differentiated. However, presently, most foremen do not participate in QC circles.

From the standpoint of improvement activities, at QC circles, there is a need for a theme which allows everyone to participate in the discussion. Therefore a theme which is too technical and difficult, or one which requires investment in capital goods and equipment, will not be suitable for such meetings. On the other hand, foremen must deal with all questions which are left unanswered by the QC circles. And in many instances, they themselves may not be able to solve these problems and must request help from engineers and section chiefs. They may also need help in their inspection activities to promote improvement.

As seen from the perspective of proper techniques, the levels of the themes adopted by the foremen are rather high. In contrast, in QC circles the same is not true. In the QC circle meetings, when a high-level technical theme is presented, we must be concerned with the fact that it may stifle full participation in the group discussion.

For the reasons just stated, I think it is wise to listen to each of these activities separately. In the Toyota group companies, we make the practice of separating meeting places of QC circles from those of foremen discussion groups.

This is an aside. At one company, foremen and other workers are joined together in small group activities. So they plan to hold joint presentation meetings. A possible danger of this type of combined meeting is that the foremen may dominate all the proceedings and thus stifle enthusiasm for QC circle type activities. On the other hand, if enthusiasm remains high and everyone will speak up, then there is nothing wrong in holding this type of meeting. In fact, it can be quite desirable.

Question 2. Is It Necessary to Have a System of Receiving Suggestions for Improvement?

In your explanation, you spoke of training each worker to submit a suggestion showing how his own work and the group's work can be improved. In our company, we do not have a system of allowing individuals to submit their suggestions. Is it necessary to establish such a system?

Answer

It is not mandatory that a system be established. In small companies, it may cost too much time and money to operate such a plan. They can end up establishing a system without being able to operate it.

It is more important to establish an atmosphere which is conducive to receiving suggestions than having a formal system. The next most important consideration is for a superior to form the habit of listening to every suggestion presented to him. To be heard is more important to employees than to receive a $10 or $20 award for suggestions.

I should like to refer to the successful innovative suggestion system established at Toyota 35 years ago. It has been utilized fully, and I attribute its success to the following factors:

1. To encourage line workers' participation in the company's improvement activities, managers and supervisors at the workplace have utilized this system fully.

2. If a suggestion is given by a subordinate, his manager or supervisor immediately implements it on a trial basis as long as the matter is within his jurisdiction. This practice of "suggestion equals implementation" has been pervasive. In some companies where a formal suggestion program is in existence, suggestions may not be acted upon until after the evaluation committee has approved them. In such companies, the program instead of aiding improvement actually hinders it.

At Toyota Motors, the evaluation committee passes judgment on the merit of suggestions less than 10 percent of the time. Most of the suggestions brought before it are there merely to determine the amount of prize, because they have already been placed under the "suggestion equals implementation" system.

3. The direct superior is always included in the first round of evaluation. For those who submit suggestions, this means that their superior is always aware of what they are doing. This system automatically fulfills one of the cherished goals; namely, that of "To be heard is always the best prize." Their desire to participate is naturally enhanced.

4. There is only a short interval between the time a suggestion is received and the time a prize is awarded. Anything submitted this month is acted on by the end of the next month. The rate of carryover to the following month is less than one percent.

Question 3. What Shall We Do When Seeds for Improvement Cannot Be Found in Administrative Divisions?

In the manufacturing processes, "defects" such as poor quality and delay in delivery are many, and improvement activities can be conducted easily. At administrative divisions, "defects" are not apparent, and seeds for improvement cannot be found. How can we handle this problem?

Answer

Each of these divisions can ask its immediate subsequent process to determine if the quality of its work is good or not. The immediate subsequent process can be another division, a superior, an affiliated factory or a customer. However, even though the subsequent process may know of the poor quality of the administrative division's work, it may not indicate that to the latter. If there is no desire on the part of the administrative division to improve, and it is good in creating excuses, the subsequent process may feel that "It's a waste of time even to mention failure to them." This is the kind of division which will always claim, "Look we are doing a splendid job. No one ever complains to us!"

To those divisions which do not receive complaints, my advice is this: "Go and ask for complaints [in the original Japanese, *chumon*, or take order] actively." Once a complaint is received, say "thank you" first and then ask: "We would like to improve our mistake immediately. Can you enlighten us further about your complaint?"

Even if a division does not go out looking for complaints, if one is received—which can even be just a remark like "Your work does not mesh well"—the first response must always be "Thank you!" If everyone in an administrative division can say "thank you" sincerely in this manner, that in itself will be a great accomplishment.

Let us now turn to the topic of cost. In the manufacturing processes, cost reduction follows reduction of poor quality products. In an administrative division, cost comes after "poor quality work" and "complaints." If the division picks up cost as its theme, it should not be too difficult to find many seeds for improvement.

Question 4. What Help Can You Provide for QC Circle Activities?

You referred to QC circle activities earlier. May I pose a couple of questions about QC circles? Some people say that QC circle activities must be left autonomous, and therefore it is not wise to assist them actively. But if you leave them alone, I fear their activities may fizzle. What suggestions do you have?

Answer

It takes a long time before QC circle activities can function smoothly if left on their own. So, initially, I suggest you provide active assistance.

There are two types of assistance. The first requires the company's involvement on a companywide basis. The second is individualized assistance which middle management can provide for QC circles organized by their subordinates.

The assistance that the company can provide is enumerated below:

1. Furnish guidelines for organizing a circle.
2. Provide guidelines for selecting the leader of the circle. For example: "During the first year of the circle's operation, it is best to name as its leader someone who has the power to command, such as a foreman or a subsection chief."
3. Hold study meetings for the leaders.

In addition, the company must also provide training sessions for middle management who must act in the capacity of advisers to QC circles.

4. Provide guidelines concerning the time and frequency of circle meetings. Guidelines showing the hours that everyone can meet are especially appreciated by those who are in service industries where frequent traveling is required.
5. Hold a general meeting for presentation on a companywide basis.

Middle management can instruct and assist in the following areas:

1. Be available for consultation on the selection of themes.

Think about several alternative themes ahead of time, and help the leaders choose the most suitable ones for their circles.

2. Help circle leaders become more effective in presiding over their meetings.

Do not attend the meetings yourself, but listen to the reports from the leaders to see how they fared in the meetings. Then give them some guidance. Make certain that everyone speaks up at the gatherings. If not, something is wrong with the manner in which they conduct their meetings.

3. Instruct and assist in the utilization of QC techniques.

Ask the leader after the meeting is over to see if he has used the QC techniques properly. Then give whatever advice is needed.

4. Instruct and assist in the formulation of implementation items.

This is of special importance when facilities and equipment are about to be renovated. When leaders come to discuss this issue, be sure to give them as much attention as you can.

As you assist these QC circles, you will see that every member will become imbued with the notion that "our work is to be improved by ourselves." Once you reach this stage, the amount of instruction and assistance can be gradually reduced.

5

Evaluating QC
Through Checklists

"**W**ill you teach us how to evaluate our own QC circles?"
I received this request one day from the president of a company where
I was serving as an evaluator of its general meeting of QC circles.
Obviously, he and other people in the company approved of the way I
made my evaluation.

By then evaluating QC circle meetings was old hat to me, so to
speak. Since 1966, I had given lectures on methods of evaluation to our
various affiliated factories. I was manager of Toyota's purchasing control division and concurrently served as an instructor in QC for our
suppliers. The QC circle idea was still in its infancy, but most of Toyota's
suppliers already had their own circles. However, they had a difficult
time stirring up enthusiasm among workers to participate in QC. Lack
of leadership was evident, and one of the priorities for me in those days
was to give leadership training in QC circles to those affiliated factories.

I could draw on my own experiences as a leader of QC circles at
various Toyota plants where I served. To study methods of evaluation,
I developed a teaching method which extensively utilized varied checklists. I used this method to train Toyota's suppliers with success.

I am pleased to note that most of the people who learned QC from
me are today directors of their own companies. The knowledge they
acquired has been transmitted to the new generation of middle man-

agers, who, in their own right, are good QC evaluators. In these companies QC is alive and well. However, only 30 companies are affected by my teaching, and they are all related to auto parts. The purpose of this chapter is to expand this method of teaching to others, inasmuch as I receive requests from other companies to serve as their instructor. May I now proceed to explain my approach?

I. Characteristics of the Checklists and How to Use Them

Basic, Intermediate and Advanced Levels

Whatever we teach, we must always teach in accordance with the ability of the learner. We cannot give a college-level lecture to a middle-

BASIC CHECKLIST

Theme: Date Checked:

Presented by: Checked by:

Item	Point to Consider	Evaluation*	Numerical Equivalent**	Note
1. Reasons for selection	(1) Why was this theme chosen? Is the reason clear to all? (If it is clear to all, that will suffice)	[ ]	(−20)	
2. Analysis	(1) Are facts ascertained through a certain method? (e.g., Pareto chart will be good)			
	(2) Better still to have the cause-and-effect diagram (but exclude from grading).	[ ]	(−20)	

Table 5-1: Basic Checklist

Item	Point to Consider	Evaluation*	Numerical Equivalent**	Note
3. Measures taken	(1) What measures have been taken? Is this clear to all?	[ ]	(−20)	
4. Results	(1) If there is something which is of use to the company, that is a positive sign.	[ ]	(−20)	
5. Standardization	(1) Do they understand the concept of "not backsliding"?	[ ]	(−20)	
Total	(100 points = a perfect score)		Pts.	

Special Items

*Evaluation—Assign a letter grade: A, B or C.

**Numerical equivalent—Deduct points in the following manner: C = −20; B = −10. For each column, the maximum number of points which can be deducted is shown in ( ).

Table 5-1 continued

school pupil and expect him to understand it. Without understanding, eventually he will lose interest in it.

The same can be said about a QC circle. Do not ask those people who have had only three months experience with QC to use intricate QC methods. Nothing can be gained by this. It may even prompt a comment from them such as: "We don't like QC. It's too difficult."

When you serve as an evaluator, it is equally important to know the level of the people or groups being evaluated. Thus I created three different evaluation checklists to match the levels attained. The basic level consists of those who have had less than six months experience with QC (Table 5–1). If they complete that stage, they enter the intermediate level (Table 5–2), and if they move up further, they become members of an advanced group (Table 5–3).

INTERMEDIATE CHECKLIST

Theme: _____   Date Checked: _____

Presented by: _____   Checked by: _____

Item	Points to Consider	Evalu-ation*	Numer-ical Equiv-alent**	Note
1. Reasons for selec-tion	(1) Improvement and main-tenance of status quo (measures against ab-normality). How clearly is differentiation made?	[ ]		
	(2) When characteristic val-ues are selected, are they clearly stated (e.g., the group's percent de-fective, and number of defectives)?	[ ]	(−15)	
2. Analysis	(1) Is the method of stratifi-cation adequate? (Is it conducted in such a way that measures to be taken can become apparent?)	[ ]		
	(2) Is the Pareto chart well drawn?	[ ]		
	(3) Is the cause-and-effect diagram a good one? (characteristic value, fishbone)	[ ]		
	(4) Is the order of analysis a correct one?	[ ]		
	(5) After testing is there a desire to study the product's utility and fit-ness?	[ ]	(−15)	
3. Measures taken	(1) Are the measures well coordinated with the analysis made?	[ ]		
	(2) When was the action taken? Do they know it?	[ ]	(−15)	

Table 5-2: Intermediate Checklist

80

Item	Points to Consider	Evalu- ation*	Numer- ical Equiv- alent**	Note
4. Results	(1) Do they use the same characteristic value originally selected through their "reason for selection" in making comparison?	[ ]		
	(2) Is it clear that the re- sults are better? (Do they have a "progress chart" or the like to indi- cate it?)	[ ]	(−15)	
5. Standard- izaton	(1) Among those for which measures were taken, have they given thought to the possibility of their returning to the original state, if left unattended?	[ ]		
	(2) Have they made changes in their manual of standards? Have they made additions to their checklists?	[ ]	(−15)	
6. Remaining problems	(1) Have they reviewed their own work and made plans for the fu- ture?	[ ]	(−15)	
7. Manner of presenta- tion	(1) Are words clearly audi- ble?	[ ]		
	(2) Are charts and graphs and materials distrib- uted easy to under- stand?	[ ]	(−10)	
Total	(100 points = a perfect score)		Pts.	

Table 5-2 continued

*Evaluation—Assign a letter grade A, B or C.

**Numerical equivalent—Deduct points in the following manner: C = −10; B = −5. For each column, the maximum number of points which can be deducted is shown in (   ).

Table 5-2 continued

ADVANCED CHECKLIST

Theme: Date checked:
Presented by: Checked by:

Item	Points to Consider	Evaluation*	Numerical Equivalent**	Note
1. Reasons for selection	(1) How well is the differentiation between improvement and maintenance of status quo made? (Abnormality control measures) (Relationship with instructions from the superior, relationship with routine management materials—are they clearly stated?)	[ ]		
	(2) Is the characteristic value selected clear to all?	[ ]		
	(3) Is the timing clearly stated?	[ ]		
	(4) Are the goals clearly stated (deadline and characteristic value)?	[ ]	(−15)	
2. Analysis	(1) Is the method of stratification adequate?	[ ]		
	(2) Is the Pareto chart well drawn?	[ ]		

Table 5-3: Advanced Checklist

Item	Points to Consider	Eval- ua- tion*	Nu- merical Equiv- alent**	Note
	(3) Is the cause-and-effect diagram well drawn (characteristic value, fish-bone)?	[ ]		
	(4) Have they given thought to the scope of utility, and degree of difficulty in control?	[ ]		
	(5) Have they adequately uti-lized correlation, differen-tials and control chart to examine testing results?	[ ]	(−15)	
3. Measures taken	(1) Are they coordinated with the analysis made?	[ ]		
	(2) In the action plan, is the deadline for action clearly stated?	[ ]		
	(3) When there are tempo-rary measures and per-manent measures, are they clearly differen-tiated?	[ ]		
	(4) Do they adequately com-municate to their supe-riors and other offices on matters which require their cooperation? (Have they consulted other of-fices about their own im-provement plan?)	[ ]	(−15)	
4. Results	(1) Do they use the same characteristic value origi-nally selected through their "reasons for selec-tion" in making compari-son?	[ ]		
	(2) Is it clear that the results are better?	[ ]		

Table 5-3 continued

Item	Points to Consider	Eval-ua-tion*	Nu-merical Equiv-alent**	Note
	(3) If, through stratification, certain measures are emphasized over others, the results of those emphasized and the overall results must both be reported.	[ ]		
	(4) When cost reduction is discussed, is the cost of improvement taken into account?	[ ]		
	(5) When cost reduction is discussed, is there an adequate checking of quality? (This may be entered under "analysis.") •In cost reduction, is it expressed in a specific amount of money? •When quality is raised, is there mention of rising cost?	[ ]		
	(6) Is the difference between main results and byproducts clearly stated?	[ ]	(−15)	
5. Standardization	(1) Among those measures proven effective, have they thought of some which may require "applying the brakes"?	[ ]		
	(2) Have they made amendments and/or additions to their manual of standards, checklists and control charts?	[ ]		

Table 5-3 continued

Item	Points to Consider	Evalu-ation*	Numer-ical Equiv-alent**	Note
	(3) Have they attempted standardization for things which fall under the same category?	[ ]	(−15)	
6. Remaining problems	(1) Is it clear to the group that some of the things they plan to do have not been accomplished, and why they have not been accomplished?	[ ]		
	(2) When they are not able to reach a goal, do they study the reason?	[ ]		
	(3) Do they pay adequate attention to byproducts?	[ ]		
	(4) After reaching a goal, have they thought about the next goal?	[ ]	(−15)	
7. Manner of presenta-tion	(1) Are charts and graphs, materials distributed and actual items effectively utilized?	[ ]		
	(2) Has the presentation been kept within the as-signed time frame?	[ ]	(−10)	
Total	(100 points = a perfect score)		Pts.	

Special Items

*Evaluation—Assign a letter grade, A, B or C.

**Numerical equivalent—Deduct points in the following manner: C = −10; B = −5. For each column, the maximum number of points which can be deducted is shown in (   ).

Table 5-3 continued

"Good Points" and "Just a Little More"

Your employees have worked very hard to solve a problem and presented their findings. Suppose you come to the meeting and say: "This part is not good at all, and that is bad too—and now look at this!" If you keep on stressing the bad points, everyone will become so discouraged that no one will want to continue to engage in QC circle presentations.

Remember that QC circle activities are not precisely the work of the company. The employees, independently and willingly, tackle those themes related to their work and want to make an improvement. Do not tell them that everything is bad to stifle their willingness.

You must provide support and encouragement to motivate employees to proceed to the next improvement project. You can do so by always praising their good points before commenting on some of the inadequate matters.

There are some people who say: "There is not a single point worthy of praise." My answer is this: "For example, if the reason for selecting this theme is clearly stated, that is the group's good point. Why not praise them for it?" But those diehards may still say: "They are simply doing what they are supposed to do. Is there any point in praising them for it?"

Actually when the employees follow the basic thoughts behind QC and QC techniques, they are doing something right, and that in itself must be regarded as their "good point." They are doing what "they are expected to do," and not everyone can do correctly what he is expected to do. For example, the reason for selecting a theme must be stated clearly ahead of everything else. Some QC circles may state their reason by saying "we somehow felt like doing it." But this is not clear. The reason must be a concrete one like the following: "We had a complaint on this matter on so and so date, and that is the reason we decided to study this theme."

This is a simple and obvious requirement, but there are many people who cannot handle it, especially if they have had less than six months of experience in QC. In my experience, about one-half of the people are unclear on this issue. Therefore if the group knows why it has selected a particular theme, they must receive praise for it. It helps to enhance their self-confidence and motivates them to move forward. The praise also teaches others to know how to handle the same issue the next time around.

You can make your point without offending QC participants. My favorite is: "If we could ask you to do just a little more (*yoku o ieba*)."

Most people use the term, "bad points" or "inadequate points," but in my many years of conducting QC circle activities, I have never used these words. If people have just begun studying QC circle activities, it is natural that they may make mistakes in the application of QC techniques and their presentation may not follow the QC story format as prescribed. It is not their fault, and if we are to assess the responsibility, it must be found in the method of instruction. I can never point a finger at the circle members and say this and that are their bad points.

I urge others who are concerned with QC to use the following expression: "If we could ask you to do just a little more." This must be said in a manner that connotes: "It was my fault that I did not teach you people adequately, and that's why you could not comprehend this point. I am going to be teaching you in a much easier-to-understand fashion. So please take note of it."

Next comes the issue of how often an instructor should use the phrases: "Good points" and "If we could ask you to do just a little more." I think two or three times would suffice for the beginning groups. To say too many things may cause "indigestion," but for intermediate and advanced groups, the number can be increased.

How to Use the Checklists

For the first meeting and possibly for the second, I use the basic checklist. My own evaluation is noted with the letters A, B and C in each column. Those columns receiving an A means they are good, and are praised as the group's "good points." Those columns receiving B or C fall in the category of "If we could ask you to do just a little more."

The job of an instructor does not end by simply saying "do just a little more." He can call it a success if the group can say: "We understand it now. We will not make the same mistake again next time around." If the group does not understand, that is the fault of the instructor. If the matter is complicated and an oral presentation does not do the job, use the blackboard. In the Pareto chart, every item must be organized according to size, with the second largest one always following the largest one. Now assuming that the fourth item is larger than the third, one drawing on the blackboard can do a lot more than a long verbal explanation.

When shall we move on to the intermediate level? That question can be answered by observing the performance of the group. The group may be receiving too many A's if the basic checklist is used when it is making its third presentation. The evaluator may suddenly find that there are hardly any B's and C's, and he has practically no column for which he can say "If we could ask you to do just a little more." That is the time to change to the intermediate checklist.

The same presentation, which has not received any C mark in the basic checklist, may find two or three such marks if the intermediate checklist is used. So by using a different checklist, an opportunity to say "If we could ask you to do just a little more" arises. When we move from the intermediate stage to the advanced level, a similar thing happens.

The illustration below shows a progress report of one QC circle which is reproduced here to indicate how the checklist system may be utilized.

Assigning Numerical Equivalent

In addition to the column which allows the evaluator to assign letter grades A, B and C, there is another column for numerical grades. At first, use only letter grades, and ignore the column for numerical grades.

You may wonder when we begin to use the column for numerical grades. This is done when we notice that the presentations are becoming better and we want to make a graph to show the circle's progress.

These numerical grades are directly transferred from the letter grades A, B and C, and need not be assigned while listening to the presentation. How do we translate the letter grades into numerical grades then? We do assign a certain numerical value to each of the columns of the QC story, and points are to be counted against those established limits. When a circle receives a number of C's in the same column, the lower limit remains a zero, so there cannot be a minus sign for this evaluation.

Readers of this volume may or may not agree with this method of assigning numerical values, but this method remains valid, and as such is worthy of your attention. Figure 5–1 shows the progress of Circle A in a graph. You can see that when the circle made its third presentation, the intermediate checklist replaced the basic checklist. When you want to make a general assessment for the entire division, the graph becomes a useful tool because you can immediately see the mean value and dispersion.

Please bear in mind that these numerical grades are still only secondary in importance. The important thing is to use the letters A, B and C to determine which part must be emphasized in the evaluation. I want to make sure that this fact is not overlooked.

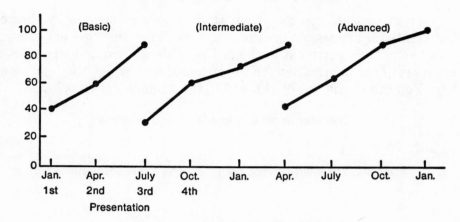

Figure 5-1: Progress Report of Circle A

II. Points to Remember in Making an Evaluation, and How to Become a Better Evaluator

Points to Remember in Making an Evaluation

There are three ways of making an evaluation. The first is to evaluate by theme (and therefore by presenter) individually, and the second is to evaluate by item. For example, evaluation is given to each of the items, such as "analysis" and "standardization." The third method is to give an overall evaluation by commenting on the entire presentation.

However, we must keep in mind that a general meeting of QC is not held frequently. To be effective, evaluation cannot be confined to the third alternative, that of an overall evaluation. A better educational result can come about if we evaluate by theme and by item.

Evaluation by theme or by item has its own strengths and weaknesses. An evaluation by theme is good for the circle under review, and will serve as a strong motivating force for its participants. However, for those who are in the audience, there is no direct bearing. They may not feel that the topic or theme has anything to do with them, and the educational value for the entire group is thus lost. But when an item-by-item evaluation is given, we have to worry about the opposite result. People in the audience can feel a certain sense of affinity for the evaluation—but to those who have made the presentation, there is often an "empty feeling," based on the fact that the evaluator has not paid much attention to what they have been saying.

To avoid this, you may want to give your evaluation by theme, but create an impression for the larger audience that you are talking about conditions pertinent to them. Use a blackboard and write down some pertinent information for the audience with which they can identify. You can divide the blackboard in the manner shown below:

Comments on Circle A's ＿＿ Activities

Good Points:

    1. Method of analysis fine, especially in its *use of the Pareto chart.*
    2.
    3.

Just a Little More:

    1.
    2.
    3.

Figure 5-2

As illustrated in Figure 5–2, the evaluator is commenting on the circle's use of the Pareto chart. He can praise the circle for drawing not just one Pareto chart, but for drawing another for the largest item showing its stratification. As he does this, he must draw an illustration on the blackboard as shown in Figure 5–3. It can make a lot of difference in the audience's perception.

An important thing to remember is that the evaluation is not just for the benefit of those circles which are evaluated. It must be presented in such a way that the audience can understand it also.

There is another important consideration. This is not an easy task, but it relates to the question of where to place the emphasis when evaluating theme by theme. Assuming that circles A, B and C all did a good job of "clearly stating the reasons for selecting a certain theme" and the evaluator dwells on that point, this can be rather boring to the audience.

What can he do then? If there are other good points in the presentation of Circle A which he wishes the audience to know, he must explain these points in detail, and say only in passing about its ability to handle the "reasons for selection" part. But when the evaluator comes to Circle B, he may wish to explain in detail why "reasons for selection" is important to QC circles. When this advice is given on paper, it looks simple. But it is a difficult task because the evaluator must make this

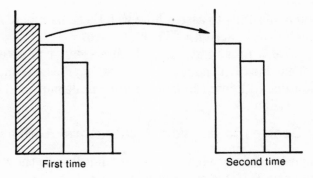

First time   Second time

Figure 5-3

type of decision while still listening to the presentations, and as soon as presentations are over he must also finish his own part of the work. He needs a high degree of technical sophistication. I should like to take another opportunity to discuss this issue, but in the meantime, I hope you will give some thought to this as you prepare to evaluate your company's QC circles.

Additional Items for Evaluation—How About Activities Themselves?

Up to now, I have concentrated on the contents of the presentation. Emphasis has been placed on issues such as "Does the circle know the QC story?" or "Does the circle know QC techniques?"

Actually there is another equally important issue. It deals with the circle activities themselves.

The purpose of the QC circle is not just to solve problems through QC and obtain results. A more important consideration is to train all the members in such a way that they have eyes to see problems surrounding their own work, can discuss these problems openly and freely with others and thereby become better motivated. Some workers may be able to make fabulous presentations. But if these talks are not accompanied by the desire to enhance circle activities, the true meaning of QC circle activities is lost.

Those who evaluate must observe and check the degree of motivation, and include it in their evaluation. We all know who the members are, how often they meet, when they meet and the ratio of attendance through the introduction given before the presentation. But we cannot always know if everyone in the circle speaks up and does so with enthusiasm. These are matters which must be ascertained through questioning. We must also try to assess how well these members will continue to engage in QC circle activities in the future.

Lately, after a presentation, each circle leader is given an opportunity to present his own thoughts as a leader. This has made it easier for the evaluators to know the degree of commitment and spontaneity among the participants.

Study Groups to Improve Evaluators' Abilities

If evaluators follow what has been said above, they can become effective evaluators. However, I still suggest that middle management as a group create a study group to help each other master the art of evaluation. Everyone will benefit by gaining greater self-assurance. This is especially meaningful when middle management members are novices in QC. This is so because one can learn the essence of QC by studying evaluation methods.

There are some companies which proclaim their dedication to TQC but conduct only QC circles. Most middle managers are left behind in QC activities at places like these. To prevent this from happening, I encourage middle managers to become evaluators and study the art of evaluation. At companies where middle managers are at least one step ahead of QC circles, circle activities are far more vigorously conducted. Naturally their companywide QC activities progress more smoothly.

Now let me provide some examples on how to promote mutual study:

Example 1

A study session is held once every other month which lasts about two hours. The meeting is chaired by either the manager of the QC headquarters, his deputy or the head of the QC secretariat.

The first meeting has on its agenda examples from the basic-level QC circle activities. They are presented either by members of the QC secretariat or by chiefs of the sections where these examples took place. The basic checklist is used by everyone to mark the good points and "just a little more." The chairman of the meeting notes everyone's evaluation on the blackboard. As discussion progresses, it becomes more sharply focused, with only two or three "good points" and two or three "if we could ask just a little more" remaining there for further elaboration. In this way, everyone is taught how to confine their evaluation to a few key issues which are "consistent with the capabilities" of the circles evaluated.

The second meeting uses intermediate-level activities as examples for study.

Example 2

In the first example, there was a chairman and everyone gave his opinion which was duly noted on the blackboard. Everything was discussed under the direction of the chairman. In this case, each person thinks about the evaluation he is going to give, and after it is completed writes down his own conclusions on the blackboard.

The blackboard is predivided into five sections, and five persons write their evaluations at the same time. They study each other's evaluation, discuss it and determine whose evaluation is the best. This method works very well with a small number of people, say five or so persons. If there are more people in the study group—for example, if there are 20—divide the group into five subsections with four each in a subsection. The subsection determines its evaluation and then transfers it to the blackboard.

III. Questions and Answers

Question 1. Can the Checklists Be Misused?

If contents of these checklists are made public, presenters may prepare ahead of time just for the sake of receiving the A rating. Can this happen?

Answer

It is not always bad if everyone aspires to receive the A rating. For example, there may be a circle which has done everything which is asked of it by the checklist, but in the process of its preparation for presentation has forgotten to include some important supporting documents. It consults the checklist, and adds the missing documents. In this case, the action is actually a commendable one.

On the other hand, there may be another circle which has never used the cause-and-effect diagram. But in order to receive an A rating from the checklist, it draws the diagram after the fact, and presents it as if it had always been used in the circle discussion. This is, of course, unconscionable. In cases involving man-hour reduction or value analysis, there are methods which are more suitable than the cause-and-effect diagram which must be used.

I have included in the checklists the Pareto chart and the cause-and-effect diagram in order to ascertain if everyone has mastered the basic QC techniques. Therefore in the initial stage, if the circle could choose themes such as defectives reduction or delay in delivery, instead of man-hour reduction, it would make the task of evaluation much easier.

These themes would allow evaluators to check the participants' understanding of the Pareto chart and the cause-and-effect diagram.

This is an aside. A section chief spoke to me about his experience: "While using these checklists to evaluate the work of various QC circles, the QC story became part of me. Whenever I make a report to my superiors about my routine work, I follow the QC story. It makes me much better organized, and I believe my superiors appreciate that too. From now on, not just when I make a report, but also when I start a new improvement activity, I plan to follow the sequence given in the QC story very carefully." This is one of the nicest things I ever heard.

Question 2. Isn't There a Danger of Presentations Becoming Perfunctory When Checklists Must Be Carefully Observed?

Your checklists are organized along the lines of the QC story, and every item contained in the lists must be evaluated. For those who make the presentation, the tendency is to place an equal emphasis on all items. What this does to the presentation is to make it more uniform but perfunctory. Are you concerned with this phenomenon or not?

Answer

In the early stage of QC circle activities, I think it is desirable that things become uniform, following the same format. Skills which the company needs must be mastered well. In the first stage of the introduction of such skills, imitation is not a bad way to start. This observation applies to QC circles as well.

It is especially important that every circle follows the outline established by the QC story format and explains everything from the "reasons for selection" to "remaining problems and planning for the future." The QC story is the order to be followed not only in one's presentation, but also in undertaking improvement measures. Stating it differently: "Do your improvement activities in accordance with the order set by the QC story. And when you make your presentation, follow the same order."

After three presentations, chances are the QC story is fully mastered. At that point, the circle may begin to emphasize some key items in their presentation. For example: "In order to emphasize analysis of causes, we shall spend 70 percent of the total time allotted for this." Or "In order to explain the process of examination and inspection of these three measures we adopted, we shall treat other items only briefly." At this level, this is perfectly fine.

Question 3. How Do You Treat Proper Techniques in Your Evaluation?

In your checklists, you do not have a column showing how well proper (engineering) techniques have been used. Don't you praise your workers for the effective use of proper techniques?

Answer

In solving problems related to the workplace, proper techniques must be effectively utilized, or else no meaningful improvement can be accomplished. When a circle wishes to analyze causes and establish countermeasures, it cannot do so without proper techniques.

Generally, we do not have to tell our workers to use proper techniques effectively. They do so naturally. Therefore, they do not receive praise for using proper techniques. Of course, when the application of proper techniques happens to be an exceptionally clever one, then perhaps a word or two of praise is in order.

I do not include proper techniques in the checklists. But please consider proper techniques to be something which must be shared in common by all items.

Question 4. Why Did You Add "QC Circle Activities" as a Separate Item Afterward?

The QC circle activities as such do not appear in your initial checklists. However, you seem to add an item to check such activities almost as an afterthought. Why didn't you include them in your checklists from the outset?

Answer

When I first started QC circle activities at Toyota Motors, there were only study sessions for foremen. The first sets of checklists were essentially a summary of points to consider which followed the QC story format. The checklists presented in the earlier part of this chapter came from those used in those days.

After several years, QC circle activities spread downward from the foreman class to the group leader class, and then to line workers. With all members participating, new goals were added to QC circle activities. At first QC techniques were tools utilized by the foreman class to solve problems in the workplace. With the spread of membership, we added the following new goals: participation by all workers in the first line of production; solving problems in the workplace by soliciting workers' opinions and enhancing everyone's awareness toward his work. Therefore, the manner in which the full participation aspect of QC is handled became an important issue. Thereafter we have always checked this point: "Do all members actively participate and speak up at the meetings?"

Question 5. Will You Please Supply Pointers for Advanced Techniques?

It is not easy to identify topics for evaluation as soon as presentations are over at QC conferences. But I shall try my best. Please give me pointers on how to approach this.

Answer

Evaluations given at QC conferences must serve the dual functions of evaluating circle activities for the members who have made presentations and educating the entire audience. Topics selected for discussion must fulfill these two basic purposes. May I suggest that you follow the four points discussed below:

1. First, you select "good points" from each of the presentations. In your checklist, an A signifies that it is good. So you choose about three items from those receiving A marks. The first one to be selected is the one in the blue ribbon category which is indeed the best and can serve as the model for others. If there are two which fall into that category, choose both of them—and if there are three, choose three. The next one to be selected is in the category of "commended for progress achieved."

2. As for the "if we could ask you to do just a little more" group, select two or three items from those which have received B or C ranking, always taking into consideration the present ability level and measures which can be of greatest help to the circle. If something can be said simply, and the problem is not too complicated, you can add another item. But when important issues are discussed, do not make them too difficult and thus cause an "indigestion" of ideas.

When a serious mistake is committed, but at the level of attainment of this particular circle you judge that teaching them about it serves no useful purpose, you may feel that it is best to remain silent. In situations like this, it is best not to ignore the problem entirely. Say to the circle: "On this particular point, let us study it again at a more advanced stage." Or "As to the use of this particular technique, please consult the QC secretariat."

3. Next comes the question of choosing which item to emphasize

for the purpose of educating the entire audience. You must first of all consider the general level attained by all. If all the circles which have made presentations happen to be in the top rank of your company, do not give your evaluations at that level. If you do, the overall educational effect of the conference will be greatly diminished.

There are always some items which you wish the entire audience to remember. Take advantage of the meeting, and select important educational items. They can be chosen from those good points or those in the "just a little more" categories. The most desirable situation is where one "good point" comes from each circle making the presentation, to formulate your important educational items.

4. The last point deals with the method of instruction in disseminating these important educational items. Remember that you want to teach the entire audience. So explain fully and in some detail, and add other examples to insure that they understand the points well. These important points, ideally, must be written on the blackboard to create a stronger impression.

I must hasten to add that the third and fourth points noted above refer to the way in which evaluations may be handled when addressing the full audience. In these I am merely speaking of approaches. I am not suggesting that you give separate evaluations aside from those you have already given by theme.

Question 6. If You Insist on Everyone Speaking Up, Wouldn't the Level Go Down?

In your talk you said that QC circles must select themes which allow participation by everyone in a discussion. If so, we cannot include technically difficult themes, and the level of themes selected will become lower. Are you saying that we must continue to deal with simple themes? When we go to conferences which are held on a nationwide scope, the themes are always on a very high level. . . .

Answer

You must avoid difficult themes when QC circles are just started. There are not too many people who can from the outset consider QC to be interesting. In fact a number of people attend circle meetings "because it is the right thing to do." For these people and for others, if the theme is on something about which they have no opinion and do not care to comment, they may say: "No thanks, next time I am not coming." So always keep in mind that "everyone speaks" is a very important consideration.

Most presentations at the national QC conference are given by those QC circles which have had at least five years of experience. If a circle is continued for five years, everyone in it masters the QC techniques, and has a high level of understanding about their own proper (engineering) techniques. In such a circle, active participation by all members in discussion is not diminished when difficult problems or themes are presented. Nor does their motivation suffer as a result of it.

In essence, an important thing to remember is that the level must be raised gradually while everyone in the circle continues to practice "everyone speaks."

This is an aside. The other day someone asked me: "Mr. Nemoto, what is the difference between your 'everyone speaks' and 'all the members participating' as described in the *General Principles of the QC Circle*?" May I comment on this?

The phrase "all the members participating" is defined in the *General Principle* as follows: "First of all become QC circle members and participate in QC circle meetings. All members must think, speak up and take action." In other words, within the phrase "all the members participating," there is a mandate that everyone speaks up, so there is no need to duplicate it by saying: "all the members participating and all the members speaking."

However, in my experience guiding many QC circles, the most unfortunate thing I have found is that not everyone speaks. The rate of attendance is excellent, but not so the rate of participation in discussion. If there are 10 members in a circle, there are always one or two people remaining silent. We want to motivate these one or two people as well as others. This is the reason why I insist on saying everyone must speak up.

Question 7. How Did You Happen to Start Helping Affiliated Plants in QC Activities?

Mr. Nemoto, I understand you began helping Toyota's affiliated plants to establish their own QC activities around 1966. What prompted you to do so? How did you begin your round of instruction?

Answer

In 1965, Toyota Motors received the coveted Deming application prize. At that time the committee of examiners gave us the following opinion: Your QC level has become an exceptionally high one. However, more than one-half of the parts you use are manufactured by your affiliated plants. There is a need to raise the level of your affiliated plants to the point where you are today. This will be an important issue for you in the coming years."

The top management accepted this challenge and, in order to begin guiding the affiliated plants in QC, established a division of purchasing control. I was selected as its first manager. At that time it was said by people in and out of the company: "Mr. Nemoto loves QC more than anything else. His appointment as manager of the purchasing control division is the right one."

How did I begin my work then? I decided to visit the 30 or so important affiliated plants on a regular basis in my capacity as manager of the purchasing control division. I solicited frank and unbiased opinions from their top and middle management. As for QC, we decided to concentrate on two major goals, which were "policy control" and "QC circle activities." What I endeavored to do was not to let these requests come from the parent company, but to let all the affiliated plants know that they were doing QC for their own benefit. They acknowledged this quickly, and we did succeed in our aim.

6

Maintenance
Control Activities:
Pointers for Dealing
with Abnormalities

I trust there are many people who are plant managers or supervisors among the readers of this book. In this chapter I shall be discussing maintenance control in the manufacturing process. The chapter contains a number of topics which are not normally found in textbooks. I hope they will be useful.

I. What Is Maintenance Control?

First I should like to clarify the meaning of the term "maintenance control."

The word "maintenance" is usually contrasted with the word "improvement." "Improvement" means to raise the level which has been attained while "maintenance" means to continue the present level.

What does the word "control" mean then? In this chapter, it includes all activities which are required for maintenance. I emphasize especially a series of activities which include discovery of abnormalities, emergency measures to be taken and prevention of recurrence. The image which the word "control" conveys here is the same control we visualize when we turn the wheel of QC's control circle.

When I say "maintenance," I interpret the word to include taking measures against abnormalities. However, at times people feel that the word itself does not convey a sense of being accompanied by action. That is why I sometimes use the term "maintenance activities." However, the phrase has not been fully accepted. So in order to make certain that everyone understands what I am saying, I am forced to use another phrase, "maintenance control activities."

An opinion is expressed that the word "control" will suffice for everything which has just been said. But that word is used widely in different contexts, including phrases such as functional control and cost control. In order to avoid confusion with other concepts, my preference is to revert back to the term "maintenance control." It may be cumbersome at times, but in this chapter that is the phrase I shall continue to use. It may be simplified by saying "maintenance" which connotes the same meaning.

II. Importance of Maintenance Control

Important customer claims against products in the marketplace can be divided into those caused by design errors and those caused by manufacturing errors. From my experience, most of those caused by manufacturing are from abnormalities in the manufacturing process.

Two important things to remember in the manufacturing process are: (1) to engage faithfully in maintenance control of the process to insure that no abnormality will occur; and (2) to act quickly when abnormalities occur. However, with regard to the first point, no admin-

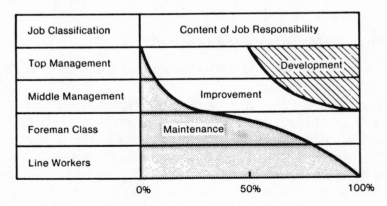

Figure 6-1: Ratio of Job Responsibilities
by Job Classification

Job Classification	Ratio of Maintenance Activities	Content of Major Maintenance Activities
Line Workers	Ratio of activities relating to maintenance, 90%.	(1) Work in accordance with the standards. (2) Discover abnormalities and report them immediately.
Foremen	Think about maintenance about one-half of the time.	(1) "Are line workers following the standards set for their work?" The foreman must inspect their work consciously and regularly, uncover work which is not consistent with the standards and correct it. (2) Discover and report abnormalities. • The ability to discover. • Make a habit of reporting immediately. Use the above two aspects to evaluate and train line workers. (3) Take immediate measures and avoid recurrence.
Middle Management	Compared to improvement activities, somewhat dull, but continue to be conscious of the importance of maintenance activities.	(1) Evaluate the ability of the foreman to train his line workers in following the standards and in taking measures against abnormalities. If such efforts are inadequate, middle management must provide sufficient training for the foreman to raise his level.

Table 6-1: Job Contents with Regard to Maintenance and Improvement Activities

istrator or supervisor seems to be very much interested in undertaking the task, perhaps feeling that the assignment is a rather dull one.

The word "maintenance" has a nuance suggesting maintenance of status quo and doing nothing at all to change things. But that is an erroneous assumption. If you do nothing, you cannot even maintain the status quo. A certain ability is required for maintenance, and efforts are always needed.

From my actual experience in the workplace, I consider the ratio between maintenance activities and improvement activities as practiced by different job levels to be close to what is contained in Figure 6–1 and Table 6–1. I hope top and middle management will use them as guides in nurturing supervisors for their workplaces.

III. Let the Workers Abide by the Standards

A supervisor's responsibility for "maintenance control" is twofold. He must "teach the workers to abide by the standards," and "be able to take measures against abnormalities." Let me explain this further.

Create Standards Which Can Be Observed

There are different types of standards, such as work standards, office standards and technical standards. These standards must be established in such a way that if workers wish to follow them, they can be followed and must last for a long period of time. There are some people who say that standards must be established on the basis of what the ideal state ought to be, or that ideally the standards must take certain different forms. However, if they cannot be observed, there is no meaning in having them.

Once I went to a company which produced defectives and inspected its manufacturing process. At that particular process, it was established that one out of every 10 pieces manufactured had to be placed in a tester to be inspected. But in actuality, 100 pieces of defectives were manufactured without interruption. If inspections were made as specified in the standards, it would not have been possible to overlook 100 pieces of defectives. Something had gone wrong.

My suspicion was that in spite of "inspecting one in every 10" as noted in the standards, that provision was not observed and in reality only one out of 100 or 200 pieces was checked. My question was answered in the affirmative, confirming my suspicion. So I probed into the matter further.

Initially, inspection was conducted three times a day, once in the morning, once at noon and another time in the evening. However, a year earlier, the company reviewed its inspection procedures and decided to increase its frequency. At that time, the company should have concurrently reviewed the cycle time (the time frame of so many minutes and so many seconds needed to produce a unit or a piece of product) and the method of inspection. This was not done, but the company still decided to increase the frequency of inspection. Under these circumstances, the workers could not observe the standards, even if they wanted to do so. They had to improvise, doing what was possible within the limit imposed. Their decision was to check one piece out of every 100. The company unwittingly imposed on its workers work standards which they could not keep.

My visit bore some fruit, however. The response to my suggestion was a positive one. "We want to change our standards into something which the workers can observe," said its top management. "We are going to simplify the method of checking. We also plan to change the cycle time. Other processes may experience a similar problem. So we are going to have a companywide review."

Standards Which Are Difficult to Observe

In the above passages, I dealt with the problem of "standards which cannot be observed." Let me now discuss the issue of "standards which are difficult to observe." I doubt there are many "standards which cannot be observed," but there are many, many "standards which are difficult to observe."

A number of years ago, a supervisor took statistical records for one month while closely observing the work of his subordinates. He was able to uncover 50 cases of work which were not following the established standards. The reasons for noncompliance are given in Figure 6-2, which contains the results of his study.

In other words, 40 cases, or 80 percent of all cases, were caused by difficulties connected with the work if standards were followed closely. For example, the manual of standards indicates that no one is to pick up anything which weighs more than 20 kilograms (44 pounds). But what is a worker supposed to do when there is no one else around? No one is there, hollering does not get any response and there is no other alternative but to do it alone. This actually happened to a worker who injured his back. If there is no one else nearby, it is unreasonable for the manual of standards to say that "two people must handle this." In cases like this, the company could make the containers smaller, and

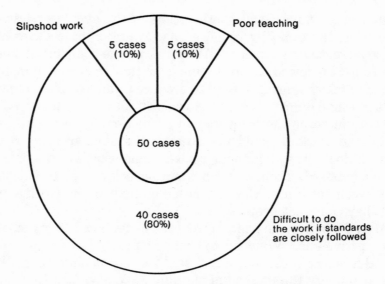

Figure 6-2: Reasons for Not Following
Established Standards

reduce the weight of each below 20 kilograms. The work standards must be modified to make them easier to observe.

When Teaching, Consider the Other Party's Receptivity and Ability

Let us now turn to the issue of "how to teach." Please refer back to Figure 6–2. According to that supervisor, five items or 10 percent of the mistakes were caused by the poor method of teaching.

Do not say, "The listener must understand when spoken to once. If he does not understand, it is his own fault." Always consider the other party's receptivity and ability, and speak in such a way that the other party can understand what you say.

Speaking of receptivity, may I share with you my personal experience? On the way back home, I played mahjong (a Chinese equivalent of a card game with 136 pieces, imported to Japan in the 1920s) with my colleagues and returned home late. My wife was at the dining table looking unhappy. "I waited and waited, and it was getting very late, so I just finished my dinner," she said. I said that I told her before leaving in the morning that I would be late because of the mahjong game. She was not placated.

I looked back to that morning trying to figure out exactly what happened. My wife always sends me off at the front door. To the side of the door we have planted peonies. That morning they were in full bloom. My wife said, "Oh, how beautiful." Come to think of it, at that very moment I said to her that I would be late. I did say it, but she was saying something else at that particular time. In others words, she was not ready to receive what I was going to say. There was no communication, and I apologized.

The next important thing is to teach in accordance with the other party's ability.

I have many occasions to speak before the meetings of managers on "the attitudes of managers." The examples I cite are carefully selected from those which can be readily understood by them. When there are more people from factories, I select examples from factories, and when there are more dealers present, I naturally select more examples from the dealerships. A speech must always have the other party's ability as a reference point. I feel complimented when people say that my talks are easy to understand. No matter how profound a speech may be in content, if there is no one who can understand it, then all the efforts come to naught.

Someone came and told me this story: "I have a subordinate who cannot understand what I say, no matter how many times I repeat the same message. So I shouted at him, 'How dare you! How many times do you insist on my making the same statement'." My response was a simple one: "Could it be that it is your way of talking which is at fault? If you continue to talk the way you do now, you will have to repeat the same thing over and over again. If the other party does not understand, try another approach." This sorry state was created because the man did not know the first thing about pedagogy.

Discovering Those Who Are Out of Sync Through "Observation"

Another important tool in insuring that workers follow standards is "observation." As a supervisor, you must observe if workers do their work the way they are taught.

I use the word "observation" deliberately, because a casual look cannot uncover what must be observed carefully.

I was at another company a few years back. There were 10 female workers doing their assembly work on a conveyor belt. I took mental note of the girl in the middle and "observed" her work. It consisted of assembling parts contained in a box twice the size of a lunch box, and after the work was completed, she was to mark on top of the box with a red pen to indicate that the work had been completed. When this was done, she would send the box to the next worker on the conveyor.

I continued to observe. She had a little extra time. After making a mark with her red pen, she stood still for a while. But later she decided to put a red mark on a box coming from the preceding process. She was taught to mark the box after her work was completed. As I observed further, she put the red mark again on a box coming from the preceding process and stretched even further to mark another box.

I called the line supervisor. "Mr. Supervisor, do you observe the work of your line workers? You may say you do, but you are probably casting a casual glance. Have you ever observed their work carefully. In five minutes of observation, I uncovered this serious deviation from standards. Suppose the noon siren just begins to wail now, and everyone goes to lunch. When they come back, they send those boxes with the red marks on automatically to the next process."

When supervisors are asked if they observe the work of their line workers, almost everyone responds by saying: "Oh yes, I observe their work the entire day." However, they only take a look at the work casually, and only a few supervisors really observe. When work improvement and process improvement activities are initiated, many supervisors use stopwatches to obtain precise timing. I want all supervisors to be at that state of readiness in observing the work they are assigned to supervise.

They are not there to see if workers are working or not. They are there to observe if the workers are following the standards as taught by their supervisors.

I shared this story with a group at another company. There they also had a similar experience.

The work called for tightening a nut to a bolt. After confirming that it is tight, the head of the nut is painted yellow and the completed piece is sent to the succeeding process. Once there was a piece without the yellow paint which was about to be sent to the succeeding process. The supervisor yelled: "Paint!" The next morning, the supervisor came to see how the work was progressing and discovered that the heads of those nuts which were still loose were already painted yellow.

The mistake occurred because there was no appreciation of why painting was necessary. After teaching how the work is to be done, the supervisor must always observe the process carefully and confirm it. I must hasten to add that when workers say "Yes, I understand perfectly," don't let the positive tone of their response fool you. Always check to see if they understand what you have in mind.

How to Question Your Workers When Standards Are Not Observed?

When you uncover incidences of noncompliance with the standards you set, how do you proceed from there?

Most supervisors will probably shout: "Why don't you do it the way you are taught?" This sentence, when written down on paper, is expressed in the form of a question, but when it is heard in the workplace, it is an inquisition. Everyone knows the supervisor is angry. And anger does not get him anywhere.

Now how would the worker feel about this? He would probably say: "Sorry, I am going to do it the way you say" on the spot. But there is no guarantee that he would abide by it afterward. More often than not, workers do not abide by the manuals because it is not always easy to do the work by following the standards set. Thus as soon as the supervisor is out of sight, they revert to their old ways.

In cases like this, a supervisor must ask the right question. "Do you see anything that's difficult to do? Let's try to change it to make it easier." If words like these are added, the question becomes a true question. But please remember, do not just mouth the words. You must truly feel that way when you speak.

In the survey cited above, the supervisor reported that out of 50 items, 40 items were caused by a difficulty in work standards. This is proof positive of the ability of the supervisor to ask the right question. If there are many types of work which are difficult to do, that must be known immediately. If supervisors do not know the true state of affairs, then it becomes a problem for the company.

IV. Discovery of Abnormalities and Quick Reporting

The term "abnormalities" as used here refers to abnormalities in manufactured goods. There are abnormalities in worker-related incidences and in facilities at a plant. These are not covered in this chapter. For now we shall concentrate on abnormalities in products.

Abnormalities in Inspection Items, Checked Items

No explanation is really necessary. If there are more defectives, or if a new type of defect is found in the checked items, these all constitute abnormalities. These abnormalities are found by inspectors in their normal inspection process, or by workers in the items to be checked by the workers themselves. If a control chart is utilized, abnormalities may be found through it. When these abnormalities are found, the superior must be immediately notified.

I need not go any further on this issue, because in most companies this issue is relatively well-handled.

Abnormalities Not Included in the Inspection Items, Checked Items

You may say, "How can we know they are abnormalities when they are not listed in the inspection items or checked items?" This is an interesting topic for discussion.

If the entire process is completely automated without any worker present, a discovery of this type is impossible. But if someone is there, that person may sense "something does not feel right" about a certain product. We ask that worker to report that feeling as an abnormality. This is to utilize effectively the remarkable "sensitivity" which man possesses.

It does not mean that we rely 100 percent on sensitivity. It remains an auxiliary tool. But a great difference emerges between those plants which give full weight to its application and those which look down on it.

Let me cite a true example. It comes from Toyoda Gosei's Inazawa Plant.

In auto parts, there is a piece called the fan shroud. It is a piece near the engine fan which has the function of adjusting air flow. It is made through injection of synthetic resins. In its succeeding process, there is a work process consisting of opening sprues and runners. An older woman who does this work one day felt that the way the plastics were cut felt quite different from other days. The feel on her hand holding a large pair of scissors was rather strange. "*Sakui*," she exclaimed. It was an unusual word suggesting that plastics were somehow soft to the touch or "easier to break." Anyway it was different.

The older woman immediately called her squad leader who in turn stopped production of the piece to examine "if the materials have somehow been changed, and if heating of the metal mold has been several degrees lower than usual." Everything else checked except the materials. The squad leader put the materials on hold and used other materials on hand to continue production. After that there was no abnormality.

In the meantime, those materials kept on hold were sent back to the manufacturer for closer scrutiny. It was found that the materials were at fault. Abnormality in the manufacturing process caused the mixing of different size grains.

The discovery was early, so the loss was kept at a minimum. This was made possible by the older woman's action, by reporting what felt "different" to her. We had never given her instructions on what to do when she found the "*sakui* (soft to the touch)" feeling. The only instruction she had ever received from us was how to cut openings. But she did report to us about an abnormality when it occurred. I was tremendously impressed by her remarkable sensitivity and by her appropriate action.

This story does not end there. On a lined, letter-size paper, her section chief wrote in his own hand a letter of commendation and posted it on the blackboard in the employee dining room. It read as follows: "This fine lady discovered '*sakui*' and immediately reported it. Thanks to her, we have been able to cut our loss to the absolute minimum. Hers is an example that others can follow. Therefore I issue this letter of commendation." On top of this letter, he wrote in a large script with chalk: "This is a letter of commendation."

Other women who saw this on the way home remarked to each other: "Now we know what our squad leader is talking about (in discovering and reporting abnormalities)."

I like this episode because it also shows how concerned their section chief is in training his workers.

Goals of Three-Minute Presentation on Maintenance

As you can see from the above, training workers thoroughly in the discovery and reporting of abnormalities is a very important task. Here are some pointers on how to create a thorough-going educational program.

The method which I describe below was first presented to Toyoda Gosei's affiliated plants in 1980 when I was still a managing director at Toyota Motors.

My suggestion was a simple one. I asked each of the factories to have its own monthly presentation session for discovery of abnormalities. At most of the QC conferences, each presentation normally takes 10 to 15 minutes, and those people who instruct in QC also provide detailed instructions. In the abnormality presentation sessions, we do not follow this procedure. Our emphasis is placed on finding materials which can be presented. Therefore, presentations are confined to three minutes, and are given by squad leaders. For example they may say: "My workers found and reported these abnormalities. And thanks to their effort, we have been able to minimize our losses." If workers do not discover and report abnormalities, the squad leader would have nothing to say in the meeting. Under these circumstances, he would have to take the matter very seriously, and this in itself promotes training on this matter. At Toyoda Gosei, we call these sessions "Three-Minute Meetings on Maintenance." There are two aspects which must be emphasized in these meetings. They are as follows:

The first deals with the discovery of abnormalities by the worker and the manner in which his or her report is received by the supervisor. When a worker finds that "something is wrong," there must be an atmosphere conducive to, or a habit formed to making a report immediately. Supervisors must all be trained to nurture this tendency in their sections or groups.

The next concern relates to "observation." We ask squad leaders and subsection chiefs to write reports stating clearly the results of their observations. This is done in order to form in their minds a habit of observing closely the work of men and women under their charge.

And speaking of the results of observation, it is not enough if the supervisor merely makes a round and says that he saw everything closely. He must be trained to report in the following manner: "As I looked at them closely, I found something which did not comply with the standards we established. When I asked why, they said that it was difficult to do the work according to the manual, so I immediately made changes, and now we can do the same task in accordance with the manual."

For a squad leader to admit discovering something which did not conform with the standards and making necessary changes is rather embarrassing. But we insist on his being able to say it in public. When all the pretences are gone, and everyone can present what he really thinks (*honne*), that marks a transition from a mere group leader into a true supervisor.

V. Analysis of Causes for Abnormalities

It is easy to make mistakes when trying to uncover the causes for abnormalities.

There was this report: "With this tester, we can only measure the outside diameter of parts. That is the cause for our creating this very unusual defective product." Can this really be true? If the tester is the cause, for as long as it has been used, there must have been many other defectives. Unless the tester was repaired yesterday, one cannot really fault it for what is happening today. We know that the same conditions have prevailed otherwise.

Something must have happened in the manufacturing process, and that must be found. In my experience, I have found that one of the following conditions is often the cause:

Change in Personnel

Personnel change can create a change in the work method which in turn can have a significant impact on the products.

One case involved a change in workers shaving off flash from forged parts. With the change in personnel, the manner of shaving off flash changed slightly. That affected the movement of a chuck in the succeeding machining process and the product's rectangular degree changed. In another example, a meter was placed in a fixed position. The work called for reading the meter while engaging in work. When there was a personnel change, a rather short person was assigned to this job. He always misread the meter by one division because the meter was placed too high for him.

When you are searching for the causes of abnormalities, get into the habit of looking into something which has changed first, and ask these questions: "Is there a change within the process?" and especially, "Has there been a personnel change?"

It is difficult for a line supervisor to report to his superior that defectives have been produced because of a change he has made in personnel. He may try to cover it up. But unless this factor is made apparent, any measure you adopt may move in the wrong direction.

Changes in Equipment, Machines and Tools

When they are newly installed, you know that fact immediately. But after their regular cleaning or change of parts during the holidays, it is difficult to know if any change has actually taken place.

You may assume that the change of parts has no direct bearing on the defectives produced this time. But the machine in question may have been tightened or loosened slightly when parts are changed. Oil may have been removed and replaced. These are changes which require some attention. Or while a machine is being repaired, those which are being processed, and those which are to be processed, may take a route different from the regular ones in flowing through the processes. This is also a change in the manufacturing process.

Changes in Materials and Parts

A hot-selling car necessitated a quick increase in production. As we did this, we discovered that some parts did not mesh well with others (for example at the point where one part meets another, and differences in their surface finish). When we checked this, we found that because of the quick increase in production, we could no longer exclusively rely on our regular parts manufacturers. We asked another parts manufacturer, which had been producing parts for a similar category car, to fill the gap. Parts manufactured by the latter met our specifications, but in a subtle way differences appeared. Our trouble came from the mixing of parts from different manufacturers.

Naturally when work standards are changed, a similar concern must also be expressed. But for now we can skip this topic.

In any event, if you want to uncover causes for abnormalities, you must always ask: "Has there been a change in the process?"

VI. Taking Emergency Measures

Here I should like to discuss the issue of taking emergency measures. For example, a welded piece was found defective after it was subjected to an inspection through destroying the piece. It was of course a sampling inspection. Now a question arises. "Have there been any defective products, similar to the one inspected, which were sent to the succeeding process, or have there been any similar defective products which have reached the customers?"

If they have already reached the customers, study must be made to determine how the matter should be handled. A report from someone who is familiar with, and can pass judgment on the problem must reach all concerned parties as soon as possible. The concerned parties may include the plant manager, director in charge of the division and manager of customer quality assurance. In any event, "the first report" must reach them as soon as possible. In situations like this, a decision must be made to appoint a person responsible for emergency measures promptly (such as a person who has the power to stop delivery).

The following happens rather frequently. "Why didn't you tell us about this yesterday? We could have stopped delivery by that much. By delaying a day, you are making our work very difficult." I am sure you have encountered similar situations. The person who is responsible for producing the defectives probably felt uneasy when he found it out. He did not want anyone else to know about it. Hoping against hope, and fearful of committing an additional error, he conducted a detailed study overnight. Well, the condition was just as expected, so he finally decided to make his report in the morning. This is, unfortunately, a scenario too familiar to all of us.

If defectives are likely to result in serious customer complaints or claims, priority is given to removing these defective products over that of trying to investigate the cause. When the "first report" is submitted, all deliveries must stop. Then begin the investigation. If results are good, then the ban on delivery can be lifted. Lately it has become easier to make the first report. In olden days, when a report was submitted, questions on all matters large and small were asked of the person making the report. To prepare for this "interrogation," he was forced to investigate everything before making his report. Fortunately, today this is no longer practiced as widely as before. But there are still instances in which we hear that an opportunity is lost because of delay.

Losing an opportunity to take countermeasures is what I fear most. This is why I insist on calling the emergency report, the "first report." If the reporter is to be interrogated on the mistakes he committed, the first report is less likely to reach there. The frequency of first reports reaching there will gradually diminish.

In undertaking emergency measures, the most important thing is to issue this first report as discussed.

VII. Questions and Answers

Question 1. Why Do We Have So Many Instances of Standards Which Are Difficult to Follow?

In your talk earlier, you said that a supervisor found 50 cases of nonconformance to the standards in a month, of which 40 cases (or 80 percent) were caused by difficulty in following the standards. It looks to me like 80 percent is quite excessive. . . .

Answer

The supervisor in question was very conscious of the fact that when noncompliance with standards occurs, there may be a problem in the standards themselves. With that awareness he made that survey, and the figure of 80 percent is the result. An important thing here is his ability to recognize that "there may be a problem in the standards themselves."

At your own workplace, I am sure you can find at least 50 percent of cases where "it is difficult to follow the standards." Please make an investigation.

Question 2. Would You Tell Us How to Create Easier-to-Observe Standards?

I fully agree with you that standards must be established in such a way that they are easy to observe. How can we make our standards easier to follow? Please give us a few pointers.

Answer

We have a couple of examples.

First, after creating the standards, the supervisor must try them out himself. If he follows the standards closely and finds them difficult to follow, then it is time to make changes in the standards.

Second, you can let the workers work in accordance with the standards, and ask them if they find any part of the standards difficult to follow. In effect, you are asking your workers to participate in the process of establishing standards, and they will be motivated to follow them thereafter.

Question 3. Do You Have Other Examples of Using Sensitivity to Uncover Abnormalities?

I am very much impressed by the story of an older woman utilizing her sensitivity to uncover an abnormality. Do you have other examples of the use of sensitivity? Are most of the examples found in the use of hands?

Answer

Indeed there are more examples dealing with the use of hands. For example: "Normally the surface is smooth, but it is a little bit sticky today." "In inserting parts with my hand, it feels lighter today. The parts are inserted too easily." Or "As I hold it, it feels a little bit heavier than usual."

Next comes the use of eyes. "The head of the bolt seems to stick out a little more." Or "The shine is somehow different today."

As for the use of ears: "When we throw parts onto the pallet, it sounds different." "The sound which occurs at the time of insertion of parts is different today." Or "The metal stamping process seems to make a lot more noise today."

Question 4. How Do You Train Workers in "Sensitivity"?

I am impressed with your talk about the use of "sensitivity" in uncovering defectives which normally do not occur. How do you train your workers to use their "sensitivity" in uncovering abnormalities?

Answer

As explained in the text, supervisors must always be engaged in training their workers to uncover abnormalities. But consider including the following approach. It is an interesting one.

When drivers of buses and trolley cars plan to make the next move, they confirm safety by saying "right correct, left correct," and they say it aloud. Let us adopt this for our own situation. If you feel something is wrong, say so. For example, "Oops, it doesn't feel right to me." Once said, you cannot leave it alone, so you may feel more like reporting the incident. What do you think of this practice?

Question 5. How Do You Utilize Control Charts?

Mr. Nemoto, when you were manager of the machining division at Toyota Motors, you made a special study of control charts and became an expert on the subject. But in talking about uncovering abnormalities, you only spoke of control charts once. Why?

Answer

I wanted to leave the issue to another occasion, but because of your question, may I add a few words.

With regards to control charts, my own thinking is as follows: Those charts which measure length and weight may be used as they are in the manner described in textbooks. Those charts which accept only numerical values cannot be used as they are, and modification becomes necessary.

For example, let us assume a control chart (*pn*-chart) is used in the painting process to analyze percent defective in painting. There are different types of defectives in painting, such as lumps, running and thinning. They look different, and are caused by variable factors. Yet in the chart they are combined, rendering it useless in uncovering abnormalities. The practice is to add up the total of defectives at the end of the day. By then, even if abnormalities are found, it is too late to take any meaningful countermeasure. Defectives have occurred more frequently in the morning. But they cannot be entered into the control chart until the end of the day. The control chart cannot flag the "abnormality" sign until then.

In your control chart pegged to numerical values, you check each item individually. The thing to do is to devise a method which would allow you to issue early "abnormality" warnings. This can be done by making modifications on the *pn* control chart as described below (Figure 6–3).

In the upper portion of this chart, whenever defectives occur they are recorded separately in accordance with the type of defectives (e.g., lumps, running, thinning and others). No column is available for entering the total. In the lower portion, a line graph showing changes is maintained only for the defective item for which special emphasis is placed. And in this chart, the line graph shows the changes occurring in the lumps.

As the workers record each incidence of defectives in the upper columns, they are able to observe the following: (1) "Today, we have more defectives than usual." (2) "Normally defectives appear sporadi-

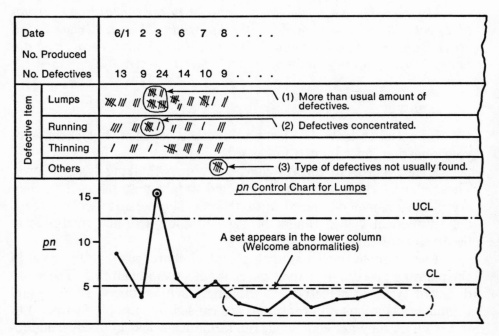

Figure 6-3: How to Adopt A *pn* Control Chart for Use

cally, but today they appear in a concentrated form." (3) "The type of defective which normally does not appear has suddenly appeared today." In this way they are able to uncover abnormalities by feeling that "Oops, something is different today!" kind of sensitivity.

Another device to use is to pile up the actual defective parts as the defectives appear, instead of noting them on the control chart. In still another experiment, the control chart is organized in a segment of two hours, instead of one working day.

With this I shall end my discussion of control charts based on numerical values. May I here deal briefly with control charts based on measured values. Once upon a time, whatever I could measure after processing, I always drafted a control chart for. But after some study, I gradually eliminated those which did not have much meaning. What I use now are mainly the following:

1. The characteristic value of the product which is delivered only after the control condition is confirmed by the control chart. This is necessary in cases involving a sampling inspection which requires destruction of the sample to obtain results.

2. In sampling inspection, the product must be taken to a precision inspection laboratory. The characteristic value of the product takes several hours to measure.

3. The relative characteristic value of a product where control of its clearance cannot be directly measured.

Question 6. How to Make Supervisors Ask Questions When Standards Are Not Observed?

Supervisors are told to ask questions whenever they discover that standards are not observed. Do you really have to make a federal case out of it? Without telling them what to do, I think supervisors will always ask pertinent questions.

Answer

Supervisors can uncover incidences of not following standards by observing—and after uncovering, they must teach their workers to correct the mistakes. The first step toward that end is to ask questions. As to how to ask questions, I indicated in the text that they must not create the atmosphere of an inquisition. Actually the issue of "to ask or not to ask" is in itself an important question.

I am sure you have had this experience also. Many of your supervisors may discover nonconformance, but "act as if nothing has happened." I asked 10 supervisors of a company to tell me truthfully how often they overlook mistakes committed by their workers. The following is the result of my informal survey:

Ten percent (once every 10 times), three supervisors; 20 percent, two supervisors; thirty percent, three supervisors; 40 percent, none and 50 percent, one supervisor (a newly appointed squad leader).

What this survey shows is that even veterans do pretend that they have not seen what they actually saw. (We can sympathize with the new squad leader, but his is not the only case.)

It is important to form a habit of asking questions immediately. Courage or willingness becomes a necessary ingredient for it.

II

FROM MEETING THE CHALLENGE OF THE DEMING PRIZE TO GROUPWIDE TQC

7

Toyoda Gosei
and the Deming Prize—
Meeting the Challenge

I. Promoting TQC—A Brief History

The First Three Years (1979–1981)

Toyoda Gosei officially began TQC in 1982, but the study of TQC was actually begun three years earlier in 1979.

The year 1979 coincided with the second oil crisis. Costs rose substantially on raw materials we were using and in some instances, they were almost impossible to obtain. We were not sure what the future held for the company, and we wanted to introduce TQC to strengthen our company's basic structure. We began by holding a series of seminars on TQC for our top management, which gradually filtered down to other groups.

In late 1979, we experienced a recall campaign caused by the poor quality of one of our products. As you are aware, when safety parts are involved in the car business, we have no other alternative but to recall cars and replace those faulty parts.

A recall campaign is an expensive proposition. But that is not all.

The goodwill and trust which took many years to build could be wiped out overnight. If the same mistake should occur again, it would mean that no further order would come to our company. We felt a sense of crisis. As we started TQC, we knew our emphasis had to be on "quality assurance of safety parts."

Actually, this quality defect was discovered by us through our regular inspection and was duly reported. There was no accident due to this defect after reaching the customer, and the damage was kept to a minimum. But as we looked into its various causes, we discovered that while the defect was created in our manufacturing process, it could have been prevented if there had been closer scrutiny at the preceding processes, such as at the stage of product preparation and the stage of design.

We extended our investigation to similar parts which were found to be defective at delivery inspection, and discovered that there were many steps we could take to insure safety and quality.

We compiled these data and organized them into an "Extended Initial Control System" as shown in Figure 7–1. We wanted to show on this diagram what each of the processes can do to help others. For example, at the product planning stage, the following questions may be asked: "What are the roles of this particular process?" "Does it plan in such a way that all performance requirements demanded by the customers are met?" In these, the process actively utilizes the quality deployment method to answer its own questions.

At the stage of product preparation, we use a checklist for fool-proofing which we call our "assurance net." We plan to make every step 100 percent foolproof. We move from one stage to another only after the Quality Council has confirmed that everything which is to be done has been faithfully carried out.

After this system was created, all important products were developed through the working of this system. The system has been in operation for six years, and during this entire period we have not had a single case of recall.

I consider this an excellent outcome for a company where more than one-half of its products consists of safety parts.

Lately we have had observation teams coming frequently from the United States and Europe. They are impressed by the thoroughness of our foolproof system for our various processes. But at the point when the initial three-year period was over, we were still not doing well as far as our companywide commitment to TQC was concerned.

We put a great deal of emphasis on quality assurance for safety

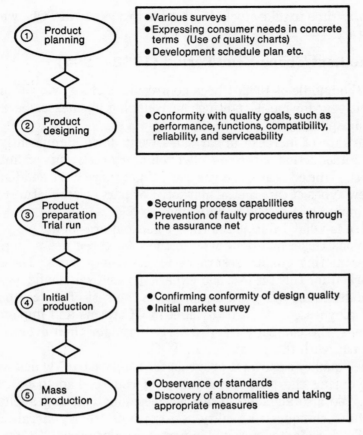

Figure 7-1: Extended Initial Control System

parts in promoting our TQC. Those people who were involved in this aspect of our movement were enthusiastic about TQC, but others were not. Therefore, a casual look would suggest that "Toyoda Gosei was not very serious about TQC."

This being the case, the level of attainment in TQC was quite uneven. I was not at all sure if all directors were ready to entertain a unified goal. In some instances, they appeared to be veering off into different directions.

It was time to take stock. If we were to succeed in TQC, we needed a new start.

The Last Three-Year Period (1982–1985)

In the middle of 1982, I became president of Toyoda Gosei. It was a difficult year for me. Conditions surrounding businesses became suddenly inhospitable.

The rate of increase in car sales went down significantly. There was the introduction of the so-called voluntary restraints on automobile sales to the United States. At the same time, there were suddenly many more new types of cars on the market. For parts manufacturers, it was the beginning of a period of suffering.

Here is what I felt at the time I became president.

Toyoda Gosei had done well in the past three years emphasizing QC in promoting quality assurance for its safety parts. Those people who worked for this project had experience and self-confidence. If this self-confidence for QC could be spread to the rest of the company, and if all employees could learn to think in QC terms and implement QC techniques, the company could emerge stronger than ever. I wanted to go ahead with the promotion of TQC.

The "quality assurance program for safety parts" which we implemented during the past three years, of course, had to be improved further. We also engaged in lateral dissemination, and applied these successful techniques to quality assurance of other general nonsafety parts. We also adopted new and important goals for our TQC promotion.

The first goal was "establishing a system of product planning." Previously we began development of our new products only after we received orders from our customers (carmakers). It was a system of receiving the order first, but would not be adequate in the coming years. We needed to know our customers' needs ahead of time, anticipating or predicting them, and developing new products independently. We needed to be able to show our customers the prototypes already developed. We had to change our system and turn our company into one which would always develop products independently.

To do so, we created a new market planning division. It was charged with developing long-range marketing strategies by product groups. At the same time technology-related divisions were given the task of establishing long-range technical development plans, and coordination of these two tasks also began.

As the president, my immediate concern was how to transfer capable people from other divisions to the market planning and technology-related divisions. I actively promoted an efficiency movement in administrative and technology-related divisions which enabled me to identify and assemble most suitable persons for these new tasks from our companywide pool of human resources.

I also served as chairman of the "conference on product planning," which met every other month. The conference served as a vehicle to determine important issues.

We also put priority on issues such as "reducing the lead time" and "cost planning."

These were the policies which we adopted, and on which we were audited in the summer of 1985, which resulted in our receiving the Deming prize.

My presentation above may sound as if we were the only ones who had promoted TQC. There were many outside consultants who unstintingly gave of their time in supporting our efforts. I want to take this opportunity to thank them for their assistance also.

II. The President Put Equal Emphasis on All Divisions

The above narrative contains Toyoda Gosei's QC promotion activities which spanned a six-year period. My own involvement as its president was during the last three years. What I tried to do was create an atmosphere conducive to the development of TQC. I should now like to discuss some of the major activities I promoted to make this possible.

Everyone Speaks

I discussed this in Chapter 1, Part I. When I first came to Toyoda Gosei, there was still a dominant feeling that "silence is golden," and not too many people were willing to speak up at meetings.

Many companies have a slogan saying "everyone participates." But that may mean to some people that their obligation is over if they attend meetings. The slogan I made was "everyone participates, and everyone speaks," with double emphasis.

There is probably no other company in Japan which has the same slogan. What I wanted to say was that my priority was definitely in this notion of everyone speaking up.

In a meeting with only 10 people participating, the rate of participation in discussion was approximately 60 percent in 1982. This was not the way to create a company with vitality. I continued to press this issue.

The atmosphere changed gradually. In 1983, the rate was raised to 80 percent, and the following year it reached 100 percent. Middle management turned into a group which actively spoke up on different occasions. For example, after the Deming prize audit was over, some of them volunteered: "I know our weaknesses are in these areas, and we are planning to take these countermeasures," or "Mr. President, may I suggest that we adopt this policy for the company as a whole?" Herein lies the wellspring of our energy and power. We are a vital company which has created the basis for its long-term development.

Interdivisional Coordination

I also discussed this in Chapter 1, Part I. After I became president, I observed the conditions existing in Toyoda Gosei and felt that there were many areas which required better coordination.

Especially in factories, it became clear to us that many of the serious problems connected with defectives created during mass production were caused by unsolved problems accumulated in the preceding processes, such as at the stages of production preparation and design. The preceding processes had their own reasons concerning this. If they had to spend too much time worrying about problems within the processes, they could not get ready for the next new product.

Factories which dealt with succeeding processes, might complain loudly to those who did the preceding processes, but to no avail. Those doing the preceding processes would normally pretend that they did not hear the complaints.

Seeing these conditions, I emphasized not only those items which were included in Chapter 1 of Part I, but also these simple concepts that "the next process is your customer," and "the first step in QC is to know if your work is satisfactory to your customer in the next process."

A section chief at a machine tool plant told me:

"We used to note on a graph how many calls were received asking us to come and fix the machines we made. We enjoyed seeing the number go down. However, the number on the graph represented only those apparent defectives. Nowadays, we send our people to other factories to ask if there are malfunctioning machines. We want to find out about all those latent complaints.

"As we start doing this, we begin to receive vital information from these factories which are helpful to us. We are now confident that the level of our manufacturing ability in machine tools is substantially higher."

Here is another heartwarming story:

"For an 18-month period, we went around everywhere to figure out how often our own technology-related divisions had created problems for other divisions. This was a first-ever attempt within Toyoda Gosei.

"As we made our rounds, we discovered that there were many instances in which no preventive measures were taken against recurrence. So we are now taking steps to standardize them."

These technology-related divisions had for some time held regular monthly meetings in an effort to promote close working relations with the plants. However, it was only after they became fully convinced of the necessity of treating "the next process as the customer," that they were able to effect true interdivisional coordination.

Concentrating on Priority Items

This is treated in Chapter 3, Part I. However, at Toyoda Gosei, the phrase "concentrating on priority items" was seldom used.

There was, for example, a division manager who insisted on including 20 items in his annual policy, for fear that too few items would make him appear delinquent in performing his duties.

My advice to men like him was: "Put only five or six items in your annual policy. Select those items for which you want to invest six months' or one year's time to complete, because old ways of doing these items somehow have not worked and you want to apply new approaches."

The managers were also asked to keep up with the progress of these carefully selected items. In drafting their annual policies, they were urged to consult with everyone connected with the affected projects, to make it certain that no one would say later: "Hey, why didn't you do what you were told."

We are living in a constantly changing world. We have to engage in new projects one after another. Yet we do not have adequate equipment or manpower. That is why we have to concentrate on only a few priority items.

Top management must also be prepared to implement the principle of "moving toward priority items" in allocating manpower, materials and capital.

When I engaged in a companywide audit of annual policies, I also utilized the concept of "moving toward priority items."

How do I select priority items? If I had time, I would want to hear everything which the workers and customers say. But time is limited, so I select some important items by asking these questions. "What is important to us?" "What are the issues we must definitely know?" "Is there anything we must be concerned with?"

Creating a "Lively Workplace" Through QC Circle Activities

Toyoda Gosei, like Toyota Motors, is a labor-intensive manufacturing company and is not a capital-intensive manufacturing company. Line workers repeat the same work from morning to night. It is not always easy to make the workplace into a place which is conscious of raising quality.

The workers receive their wages by performing their work in accordance with the work standards set for them. How can we expect them to have a highly refined sense of quality, or even maintain such an idea. For these people, it is often wise to create some occasions when they meet together to discuss the ways and means of improving their work: "Can we do this one better?" Let those occasions be jolly ones. The ambience thus created can be an important factor in motivating them further.

With this in mind, QC circles at Toyoda Gosei have always been "noisy and jolly." It is our hope that the workers learn to use the QC techniques while having some fun.

No matter how good a report may be at the presentation meeting, if improvement activities have been conducted by only two or three people and other members have not been involved, the circle is worth very little to Toyoda Gosei.

In some companies which are closer to capital-intensive type manufacturing, the foreman class and normal QC circles may join together to form another type of circle. That is fine as long as the position of the new circle is clearly defined. At Toyoda Gosei, we prefer to separate presentation meetings which are attended by the foreman class and staff, and those sponsored by QC circles. We do not want to commit the mistake of using the same criteria in judging these different types of meetings.

For example, when the foreman class and normal QC circles get together to have a joint presentation meeting, the former will probably insist on engaging in and presenting only those projects in which a larger amount of savings can be realized. Assuming further that evaluation will be based on the amount of money saved, then most of the QC circles will be quite discouraged.

Money is not everything—and the primary consideration of QC circles must be their ability to stimulate workers in raising their consciousness toward improvement, which they can do by having a noisy and jolly meeting in which everyone speaks. I prefer to see shining eyes on the faces of these workers over the amount of money saved.

III. Questions and Answers

Question 1. Can You Say Management Equals TQC?

As I listen to your discussion of TQC promotion, I get the impression that all important management decisions are made with the help of TQC. Does it mean that management can be equated with TQC?

Answer

Many experts on QC have differing opinions on this issue, and the same holds true among managers.

As for me, I consider TQC to be a tool of management. It is an important tool which covers most aspects of a company. But management does not equal TQC.

There are certain areas of management which cannot be covered by TQC. Some decisions can be made only by top management which must make its decision even when there is no adequate information or documentation. There are some decisions which require complete secrecy. There is no doubt in my mind that in management not all problems can be solved with TQC. Recently Mr. Eiji Toyoda, Chairman of the Board of Toyota Motors, published a book entitled *Major Decisions* (*Ketsudan*) (Tokyo, 1985). In it he describes in some detail the events leading to the merger of Toyota Motors and Toyota Motor Sales. That process cannot be explained through TQC, nor can TQC really take part in it. That is a typical example of a decision rendered by the very top.

In other areas of decision making, only a few need be consulted. This includes increasing capitalization, personnel decisions relating to company directors, measures for the settlement of accounts and steps to be taken at the stockholders' meeting. These considerations cannot be published as part of the company's annual policy or issued in a published document.

Oftentimes, executives say they do not like TQC because of the notion that "management equals TQC." To these executives, I have often used the above examples to give my interpretation. They usually agree with me, and then proceed to listen to what I have to say about TQC.

Question 2. What Are The Major Accomplishments of Your Three Years of TQC Promotion Activities?

In this chapter, you have concentrated on the aspect of TQC promotion without stating the many accomplishments you have realized. I am sure you have had many such accomplishments since you became president. If you were to choose five from your many accomplishments, what would they be?

Answer

If I have to choose five, the following must be mentioned:

(1) The company as a whole has become strengthened in its resolve to entertain "long-term strategic goals."

We have organized our product planning system, and we have coordinated our long-range sales plans with our long-range technical development plans. We have become sufficiently motivated in trying to coordinate all our other long-range projects which have not been adequately coordinated before.

(2) The company has become thoroughly imbued with the notions of "quality is the ultimate" and "quality first."

We have always endeavored to build in quality at the stage of development planning. In addition, we have also been able to make a significant improvement in our manufacturing processes in our plants. This has contributed greatly to the company's overall performance.

(3) Coordination between divisions has improved dramatically.

"Stretch your hands toward each other even farther than you may normally do," and "The next process is your customer, so always pay close attention to their satisfaction" are two phrases I constantly use to impress upon Toyoda Gosei employees about the need for interdivisional coordination. Nowadays, I see instances of the preceding process going to the subsequent process to hear the latter's "latent complaints." Coordination between divisions has progressed far better under TQC than I had originally anticipated.

(4) We have been able to implement "everyone speaks" and create "a lively workplace."

One of the company's slogans is: "Everyone participates and everyone speaks." As we have emphasized active participation through saying something, the rate of speaking up at meetings is now 100 percent. What pleases me most is that we now have our employees' "honest to goodness" truthful views. They also speak up positively and constructively. This vitality is going to aid the company in its future development.

(5) In the process of being audited for the Deming prize, everyone has worked hard to master the techniques of TQC. This is what the best in "human resources development" can offer.

The QC techniques which they tried so hard to master have now become part of them. They can never forget them, as these techniques have been drilled into their subconscious minds through daily practice. These techniques are useful not only to the employees individually, but also collectively for the company and for a long time to come.

Question 3. Have You Encountered Any Harm Coming Out of TQC Promotion?

So far, you have spoken of your accomplishments. Has there been any noticeable adverse effect? If so, please give us an example.

Answer

As mentioned earlier, my credo is "improvement after improvement." Therefore I also look for a better way of promoting TQC than the way we have been doing it before.

However, I believe your question is directed to issues such as: "To prepare materials for TQC, I had to go to my office on my off days," and "Thanks to TQC, our labor cost has risen and profits have fallen." These issues have been written up from time to time by the mass media.

At Toyoda Gosei, too, during the last six months prior to the Deming prize audit, we experienced the phenomena of overtime lasting long hours and coming to work on off days. These sessions were held not just for preparing materials, but also for discussing measures to be taken in correcting our weak points. This was an enormous sacrifice for everyone concerned. For the company too, it meant a substantial increase in our labor cost, since we had to pay overtime for those who were at the level of subsection chiefs and below. Those who were at the level of section chiefs and above, however, received neither overtime nor supper money.

I knew that all of these things would happen ahead of time, so I never felt that they would become impediments to our company. People who do not approve of TQC would like to pick out these incidents and create a negative image of TQC. But I consider these costs incurred as nothing but the tuition payment for our own betterment.

Individually, for some employees, these activities could have been a painful experience physically and mentally. With the increase in our labor cost, it also meant that the company would also have a smaller profit. But we planned everything ahead of time, and as president, I never felt that the decision to engage in TQC was a mistake.

Your question may also be hinting at a possibility of people becoming overeager and neurotic about TQC. And you may want to ask us if we actually have developed a case of neurotic behavior here at Toyoda Gosei. A few words of explanation are in order.

No, we are fortunate in not having a single case of neurotic behavior. We have carefully prepared our educational plans, and we have never demanded of our employees more than their abilities would bear. My emphasis has always been "to teach employees according to their abilities," and "to teach in accordance with their understanding."

When QC presentation meetings are held, I continue the practice of commenting on "three good points" and using the phrase "if we could ask just a little more" concerning two problems. Disregarding a person's ability, and picking at the manner of his presentation is not the right way to encourage human resources development.

My hope is that everyone who is involved in TQC will say: "Am I ever glad I am part of TQC," and "Gee, we now have the Deming prize." We have not had a single case of neurotic behavior. This is due in part to the fact that the employees understood my views just expressed and that I had full cooperation of my middle-level managers in this regard.

Question 4. What Are the Tasks Remaining After the Deming Prize?

While you were working toward obtaining the Deming prize, your company also experienced two profitable years in 1983 and 1984, with an increase in revenue and profit. What are the tasks remaining for you?

Answer

In our long-range planning, we have been able to coordinate our sales and technology development activities. However, we have not been able to have these activities coordinated with other long-range plans.

For example, our long-range plans for manufacturing processes and for personnel have not been adequately coordinated with our long-range marketing plan. Coordination of these plans thus becomes the most important remaining task for us. Among the changes in business conditions, issues surrounding international trade are the most serious.

Thus we have adopted "a system of training personnel in international business" as one of our priority goals. Initially, this was included as part of our long-range human resources development project. But with the suddenly changing conditions, we decided to establish a new implementation plan in the middle of the year. There is another issue which may be more appropriately placed in the category of "lateral dissemination" rather than treating it as a remaining task. We are planning to raise the level of our suppliers and make our groupwide companies stronger. We plan to establish a groupwide TQC program, and the subject will be treated in Chapter 10.

Question 5. What Is the Relationship Between the Toyota Production System and the Deming Prize Audit?

Did you put the Toyota production system up front to be audited when you applied for the Deming prize?

Answer

Our entire plant is operated on the basis of the Toyota production system. So there was no question of whether or not the system should be brought out up front. At every one of our plants, we use both the Toyota production system and QC-type approaches and techniques. Thus without our planning to, the Toyota production system would come naturally up front on its own.

Twenty years ago when Toyota Motors was audited for the Deming prize, its plants were already utilizing the Toyota production system. But at that particular time, the auditing method was on the verge of changing from statistical quality control to TQC, so we hardly used the term "Toyota production system." This time at Toyoda Gosei, we wanted the examiners to see our comprehensive approach to quality, cost and delivery. To do so, we showed how the Toyota production system and QC were combined in our total operations.

Question 6. Did You Insist on Exposing Your Own Bad Points at the Time of the Deming Audit?

Mr. Nemoto, you always say: "Actively expose the mistakes you committed. In doing so, you can help promote your own improvement activities." Did you do it while you were audited by the Deming prize committee?

Answer

When I say that all bad points must be exposed, I have in mind, how a company or its top and middle management may find seeds of improvement in the company. But the auditing for the Deming prize has a different purpose. So I did not actively present the bad points we had.

The Deming prize is awarded to a company who can utilize the QC approach and techniques, and the audit is conducted in part to determine the degree of their effective utilization. Its purpose is not to determine what the bad points of a company may be. So I did not go before the committee to say we were inadequate in this, and poor in that. It is true that in a QC story, we begin with an explanation of what is wrong with us. But the emphasis is always on how effectively results have been attained. You may have asked this question to point out how difficult it is to shift from one way of doing things to another. Yes, it was not easy, and this was one of the problems we had to work hard to overcome.

Question 7. Isn't It Inconsistent to Say "Clarify the Degree of Imperfection" and "Accentuate the Positive Points in Other People"?

In QC it is often said that the first lesson is to clarify the degree of imperfection. At an education-related meeting I attended, I was told that it was important to realize the positive aspects of individuals before true education could begin. These two thoughts seem to contradict each other. What is your view on this?

Answer

To find and clarify the degree of imperfection in a company is to find an opening for improvement in that company. If this is not made clear, we do not know what measures to take, and later when we must confirm the results, we do not know how to evaluate them. Therefore in a company, when you begin an improvement project, you must show the degree of imperfection.

What you have heard at the education meeting probably relates to the nurturing of individuals. When we teach individuals, we cannot always point out their shortcomings, and make them feel that they are good for nothing. If we do so, the person who felt slighted would lose interest in education, and become a dropout from society. Everyone is different, but each individual has a certain area in which he excels. An educator must praise it and help that person to grow in that area. That is education and nurturing. Education is not to give lectures. It is a means of expanding an individual's innate abilities.

Of course, if there is something which an educator wishes to correct in an individual, he must do so with patience. He must not cause the person affected to lose interest in education. That is the true way of education. I do not find any inconsistency in the two concepts just discussed.

Question 8. How Do You Make Sure There Is No Drop-out from TQC?

In the January 1986 issue of Statistical Quality Control, there was an article on the characteristics of Toyoda Gosei's TQC. One of your managing directors was quoted as saying: "Mr. Nemoto does not saturate us with knowledge all at once. He leads employees step by step and moves them forward in accordance with the increase in their abilities. He wants them to master QC thoroughly. Even if there are five points which are not precisely QC, he considers their ability to understand first and teaches only those matters which fit their level. I don't think there is a single individual who does not like QC who is trained by Mr. Nemoto." Is this the way you conduct your TQC training?

Answer

May I share with you my educational philosophy which predates my QC days?

An employee does his best in giving his presentation. But if you comment that "There is not a single thing to be commended in this report," you take away his motivation. Likewise if you say to him, "It is bad here, it is bad there, it is bad everywhere," his response is likely to be: "I don't want any more of this improvement nonsense." The very fact that he wanted to participate in the improvement activities in itself is worthy of commendation. You must not expect too much at first and point out too many mistakes committed by him. Teaching can be effective, if it is consistent with the ability of the person receiving instruction. That is a basic principle of education.

In promoting TQC, a similar consideration applies. However, there is one exception. If people are quite advanced in TQC, you may not want to remain silent when some mistakes are committed, because you do not want your audience to think that your silence is your implied approval. You can say it nicely in this fashion: "We cannot deal with this issue in detail today. But may I suggest that you consult the staff and restudy it. I know it will become even better."

Question 9. Where Do You Place Emphasis on QC Training?

You speak of getting to know the QC approach thoroughly and practicing it. I infer from this statement that you do not just give lectures, but you insist that your employees and others practice what they learn. Is this where you place your emphasis?

Answer

Yes, indeed. In the spring of 1985, a TQC study team came here from the United States. They asked me about TQC training. In America there seems to be a notion that "education equals lectures." I wanted them to know that I had a different view of this.

Lectures are of course necessary. But we must pay closer attention to the practical education which follows. What is learned must be experienced before it can be said that one is educated. "If a person experiences it, it becomes part of him. He will never forget it for the rest of his life. This is good for him and is good for his company." That is the way I teach.

Question 10. Do You Have Pointers for Other Presidents Who Want to Be Audited for the Deming Prize?

In your answer to Question 3, you indicated that for a period of six months, your middle managers participated in study sessions held on off days. I also understand that you, yourself, participated in many of these meetings. That was rather taxing for you, wasn't it?

Answer

In the study sessions where we had outside lecturers, it was common for the president to attend. However, in meetings which did not involve outside lecturers, I frequently attended study sessions held by our key people and staff members.

My feeling was that these study sessions provided me with unusual opportunities to observe the conditions and levels of various divisions and sections. I probably participated in these sessions several times more often than other presidents.

For other presidents who want to study TQC and prepare their companies for the prize audit, my suggestion is that they participate in those sessions where there are outside lecturers. It is not necessary to attend those sessions devoted to statistical quality control, however. It may not be easy to comprehend, even if you spend an entire day sitting in its midst.

People used to tell me that QC had become second nature with me. So I just love to attend these study sessions. But people are all different. Some presidents may feel that two or three days of study of TQC is all they can take. But they still want to promote TQC. What they must do is get a feeling for the most important aspects of key issues. They need not attend all the sessions. We do not want to have the presidents taken ill because of TQC.

There is one more thing I wish to call to your attention. Do not devote all your time to study. You need exercise also. I like QC, so there was no mental anguish when we were audited for the Deming prize. But I was missing a lot of exercise. Some people say that the last year before the Deming prize does not allow you to play golf. That has an element of truth, but we must endeavor to reshuffle our schedule to "no golf for the last month," perhaps.

Question 11. What Are the Results of Promoting Efficiency in Administrative and Technology-Related Divisions?

I understand that you actively promoted efficiency in these divisions after you became president. What are the results?

Answer

My interim report for this project covering our first six months is given in Chapter 2 of Part I. In the first 18 months, we attained about 30 percent higher efficiency, and thereafter we were increasing our efficiency by 10 percent each year.

In the past, we used to have requests like the following: "Quick, we need a person right now to fill the position vacated by someone who has just retired." After receiving this request, the personnel division would have to scramble. But seldom do we hear such a request now. Compared to the past, it is also much easier now to transfer people to priority divisions on the occasion of our regularly scheduled transfers.

The other day, a president of another company came and I said to him: "Our program continues to promote a 10 percent increase in efficiency each year." He asked: "Does it mean that in the end, you will have only one person left for a set amount of work?"

When I say that we must promote a 10 percent increase in efficiency, it means that we do work regularly done by 10 people with nine people now. If the work of the company does not increase at all, we must then reduce personnel in the administrative and technology-related divisions. However, at Toyoda Gosei, we plan to add new work each year. We plan to assign the new work to those people who are withdrawn from their old work through our efficiency movement. So there is no possibility of only one person remaining in a workplace.

Question 12. How Far Has Toyoda Gosei Gone with Its Product Planning?

I should like to ask a question about your product planning. Do you intend to cover only those groups of products you already have, or do you plan to add something entirely new?

Answer

The answer is both. If you ask which part dominates, it is the existing groups. Unlike other companies, we manufacture automobile parts for carmakers. I do not expect the present product groups to disappear suddenly one day. Thus the most important task for us is to develop more attractive items for our existing product groups.

Question 13. What Is the Difference between a Series of New Products and Safety Parts?

In the January 1986 issue of <u>Statistical Quality Control</u>, one of your directors indicated that your company had to work extra hard for a series of new products at their takeoff stage. I understand that Toyoda Gosei has an extended initial control system for safety parts which has been developed as your top priority project. Do I hear correctly that this system is not working when it comes to creating a series of new products?

Answer

The extended initial control system aims at quality assurance in the product planning and design stages and carries it throughout the process. For example, hoses made of new materials and rubber capable of withstanding vibration and having new capabilities are all placed on this system for development. On the other hand, when we speak of a series of new products, we do not develop many totally new items. The series is characterized by a large number of different parts and strict adherence to the delivery date.

When there is a model change for a car, each time it occurs there are changes in parts consisting of 300 to 500 items. To meet that schedule, manufacturing of metal molds and preparation for special manufacturing lines must be completed before the trial run is made. Making every system go is not an easy task, but through hard work we have done it. Carmakers commend us for creating a "model system for takeoff."

Question 14. What Is Your New System for Takeoff Control?

In your response to the preceding question, you spoke of creating a new system to make the takeoff process for a new series of products easier. Please give us some ideas on how this system operates, if it does not violate your industrial secrets.

Answer

Let me give you some examples of how we have improved preparation for production through the use of this takeoff system for a new series of products.

Our production preparation is coordinated with model changes for cars. Today we have a variety of products which are numerous in number. With this the processes have also become varied. For any new project, there are always many divisions which are connected to it. Another characteristic of today's process is that there are frequent design changes before we can start mass production. To meet these changing conditions, we have initiated many improvement projects. May I now cite an example from computerization of our daily routine control?

We have named this system of controlling daily routine for production preparation, START. It has as its goals the following:

1. Sharing of daily routine control data by all divisions responsible for the project(s).

2. Ability to see minute-by-minute movement of the project's progress through the online hookup, and speeding up of actions to be taken.

3. Efficiency in the office work for production preparation (man-hour reduction in control-related office activities).

Figure 7–2 shows a general outline of this system.

With the utilization of this system, all the divisions are now able

141

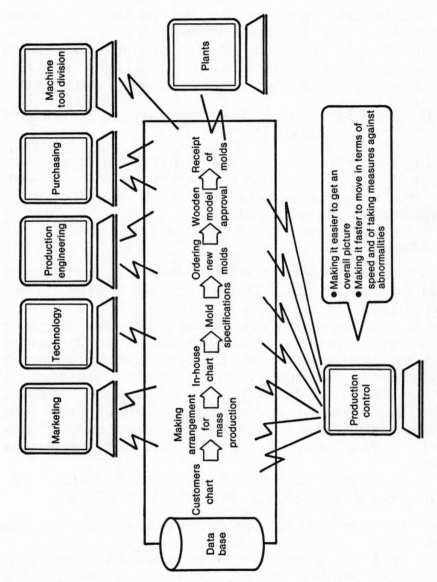

Figure 7-2: Computerization of Daily Routine Control

to share the data, and in addition we have found the following advantages:

a. It is now easier to know the day-to-day changes in production, and the system also prevents troubles from occurring due to discrepancies in the master lists kept by separate divisions.

b. We can now anticipate delays in taking appropriate actions, and are able to take measures quickly when progress is abnormal.

We plan to expand this system further, and move from man-hour reduction in individual offices to creating offices without paper.

Question 15. Who Determines Items for Companywide Audit?

You set priorities in the items to be audited on a companywide basis. But who determines the items to be audited? Is it the responsibility of the president?

Answer

The management planning office which serves as the secretariat for the companywide audit first asks the chairman and the president about the items in which they are interested and for which they want to have more information. Next, the office selects its own priority items which have been delayed in implementation by checking them against the policies previously established. Next, company directors in charge of divisions are asked to submit those items on which they want to make a report. Finally, the president selects items from the list prepared by the management planning office in this fashion.

Question 16. How Do You Use In-House Broadcasting to Check Work Standards?

It is remarkable that you have had no recalls in six years. You must have a special method of observing work standards in your manufacturing processes. Is it true that you use in-house broadcasting for this purpose? Can you tell us more about it?

Answer

The in-house broadcasting was begun at our Haruhi plant last year. And because of its success it is adopted by other plants. It works this way. At the Haruhi plant, work standards are systematically checked by using checklists at 11 a.m., and 4 p.m. At these appointed hours, an attractive female voice announces: "It's time for checking our work standards. All supervisors, please have your checklists ready and follow the plan set for today. I have a request to make of those of you who are working. If there is something which is difficult to do, please do not hesitate to mention it to your superior."

The last part of this broadcasting is unique, and is probably the first of its kind in Japan. Supervisors are asked to note and take immediate action when matters are presented to them. By the way, before the announcement, there is a short program of music. The music is selected by those who are in charge of the broadcasting who consult each other and change the program every day.

Question 17. What Do You Plan to Gain from Your QC Circle Leadership Study Group?

I understand that you have a QC circle leadership study group which meets once every month. What does the study group do? What do they study?

Answer

Two years or so ago, I compared our plants and evaluated their levels of attainment with regard to QC. I discovered that the level varied greatly from plant to plant. The one which had the worst record was the plant doing work on resin and synthetic resins. The plant expanded its operations very quickly. It had to deal with problems relating to constructing a new plant, transferring its personnel, reorganizing and restructuring its processes. It did not have much time left to devote to QC circle activities.

For a company which was intent on obtaining the Deming prize, unevenness of this nature could not be allowed to persist. We had a total of six plants at Toyoda Gosei. Of these, four were doing very well. If their ability could be transmitted through lateral dissemination to the remaining two, the problem would take care of itself. Yet these two weaker plants had many problems which were not just confined to QC circles. I did not think it wise to force QC circles upon them. I wanted them to be able to come to the following conclusion on their own: "Under these difficult conditions, what can we do to approach the level of other plants?"

I formed an ad hoc team consisting of assistant plant managers who were also serving as QC instructors. The plant with the most problems was represented by an assistant plant manager who was the oldest person in the group. I made him the team captain. I thought to myself, if this weakest plant could come close to the average, I could then disband this team.

Their study team met once a month, but rotated its meeting place from one plant to another. They would first attend a QC circle meeting held at the host plant and hear their QC presentations before starting their own discussion. The reaction to this approach was highly favorable. Even those plants which were strong in QC circles felt: "This study group is very useful. We have never had an occasion to study about other plants' QC circles in this fashion." Their enthusiasm was shared by others, and those which were weak had to work even harder. Those weaker plants were under difficult conditions, but they received much friendly advice from others who were in the study group. Soon their programs were also progressing rapidly.

The weakest plant was the Inazawa plant. It suddenly became a vital center of QC circle activities, and during the past year held two QC circle festivals at the public hall of the city. The public hall was filled, showing the enormous enthusiasm they had toward QC. I commend the executives at Inazawa and all the rest. But I also want to give credit to the study group which helped to bring about this success in an unobtrusive manner.

Question 18. Don't You Create Problems for Yourself, if You Let the Best and the Brightest Go for Rotation?

You wrote in Part I that your best people may be rotated. If you let your best ones go to other divisions and as a result your own division's performance goes down, you lose out in the end, don't you? You may even be scolded for the poor performance of your division. That doesn't pay, does it?

Answer

I evaluate a division's accomplishments along with its ability to recommend their best for rotation.

Sure enough, if the best people are kept within one's own division, that division will continue to perform better than others. I try to see how well the rest of the division can do without their best people. I want to see if they can give their utmost. I do not try to evaluate a division by simply observing its short-term results. I do not say anything derogatory to them. This is the secret to the success of a long-lasting rotation.

Question 19. What Is the Purpose of Training Internationally Minded Workers?

In response to Question 4, you spoke of training internationally minded workers. Does this refer to those people whom you plan to send overseas?

Answer

Of course, if needed we plan to train people who can be sent overseas. But I also want to train our planners who are at home to have a sense for international development and can plan accordingly. In the case of engineers, I want them to be able to go overseas and render technical assistance. But I also want them to be able to chair a panel wherever an international conference may be held. I want our people to reach that level of international sophistication.

Question 20. Can Observation Teams from America and Europe Understand TQC?

As Toyoda Gosei becomes better known, you have to host teams from the United States and Europe, coming to observe your TQC. Can they understand it and take back something of TQC with them?

Answer

My practice is to give a talk on TQC which is then followed by a visit to our plants. The visiting teams can understand clearly why TQC has been instrumental in making our company what it is today.

However, those people who came to visit were often not presidents of their companies. Many of them said they did not know how to persuade their presidents to adopt TQC once they returned home.

On the other hand, once I had a CEO come to visit us. Later he came again with 20 of his directors and division managers. In a company like that, I know TQC will succeed.

Question 21. When You Spoke to Grade School and Middle School Teachers, Did You Tell Them About TQC?

I understand that school teachers from Toba city in Mie prefecture came to visit you and heard your speech. Did you speak on school education and TQC?

Answer

The Mayor of Toba, Mr. Hamaguchi, was a former vice-president of IBM Japan and is an old friend of mine. One day Mayor Hamaguchi called me: "Can you give a speech to help us improve our office procedures and educational undertakings? Just to state your views will be very helpful to us. Can we visit you at Toyoda Gosei?" I could not say "No."

I have never studied the implication of TQC in compulsory education, so I could not speak on the theme of "TQC and public education."

However, "improvement after improvement" has always served me well as a theme, so I spoke on that subject. I wanted to share with my audience my views on improvement activities in companies and how this approach could be utilized in school education. I emphasized the following five points:

1. When your students cannot understand what you are saying, that is caused by your poor teaching. Think again how you want to explain the subject under discussion. In companies, if what we say cannot be understood, it can cause defectives and delays in delivery. We make doubly sure that the other party always understands what we say.

2. When you want to teach or give directions, if the students are absent minded or not interested in hearing what you are saying, whatever you say to them does not constitute an education. This holds true for company managers when they speak to their subordinates.

3. Some teachers may say: "I yell at my students for the sake of education." You cannot get angry and become emotional. That is not education. You must remain calm, always thinking how you may approach the students better, so they can comprehend.

In the olden days, I used to hear my colleagues say rather boastfully: "Oh, those young characters. I told them off. Boy does it make me feel good." If the old "badger" wanted a cure for his own stressful conditions, he should have gone to a bar and sang on *karaoke* [a music-minus-one device which allows singers to have a full orchestral accompaniment] and that would serve the company better. Those people who were scolded probably would have said "boo" in their hearts. That kind of scolding serves no one, and that is not education.

4. Don't shout to your students: "Do you understand?" If you do, of course, they will say "yes." When you hear this response, you think that they understood what you have just said, but of course you are

wrong. Your shouting is a command and not a question, so they say "yes" almost as a reflex. It does not mean: "Yes, we understand."

In school or in a company, this practice must be avoided.

5. Practicing for sports and working for a company are two basically different undertakings. In sports, we learn to exert our bodies to the limit of their endurance and to acquire skills, always under the watchful eyes of our coaches. In a company, we must work long hours without any direct supervision. In sports, practice sessions can be accompanied with loud shouts and cheers, but this cannot apply to work in a company.

Maybe someday this difference will become evident to teachers. When a teacher doubles as a coach, he may become confused in his two functions.

8

Fundamentals of
Total Quality Control:
Taking Stock of
TQC One Year Before
the Deming Prize

I. Speech of the President and Its Summary

I gave a speech to all of our section chiefs in 1984 as part of our observance of quality month. I had given talks on how to approach QC from time to time, but this two-hour speech represented the sum total of my own thinking, and it was intended to serve as a comprehensive review for those who attended.

Reproduced below is a summary of that two-hour speech.

Attitudes Toward TQC

(1) Improving managerial ability.

As managers and administrators, the higher one goes up in position the greater is his need for managerial ability. Between those section chiefs handling technical matters and those handling office routines, the ratio may be somewhat different. But on average, at the level of section chiefs, management techniques and proper techniques (e. g., engineering) are about 50 percent each as demonstrated in Figure 8–1.

(2) Unusual opportunity.

TQC provides an unusual opportunity for mastering management techniques. This is especially so when the entire company is geared up to be audited for the Deming prize. There is no better time to learn than at this time.

Of course, you must continue to develop your proper techniques, but this is the best time for you to learn management techniques. Do not miss this excellent opportunity, and do your very best.

The ability thus acquired becomes your own and stays with you for the rest of your life. I am sure it will be a gratifying experience for you.

(3) The areas covered by TQC.

When you study the approaches and techniques of QC, you will find your management techniques have improved substantially. In most instances, QC can serve as the tool for solving problems. As for the Toyota production system, QC does not provide an opportunity for its

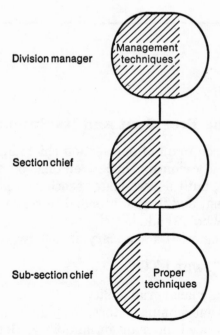

Figure 8-1

training. So we must set aside special sessions independent of QC to study it.

We sometimes use the word TQC to include instances in which we set aside new programs for training purposes. But the Toyota production system is not even included in the so-called seven tools of QC. Therefore it must be treated as a separate entity. Yet if we adopt the definition that "TQC utilizes anything which is useful," then one day we may see the Toyota production system included in QC seminars.

Ultimate in Quality (Quality First)

(1) Reduction of defectives within processes.

Since 1980, we have had no single instance of recall, and our customers' acceptance inspection for defectives is now expressed in terms of ppm (parts per million). However, in some of our processes, there are still defectives which come to several percent.

So far we have not been overly concerned with this rather high incidence of defectives, and have not established a stringent goal for ourselves. This is due in part to a feeling that when compared, we are doing as well as any of our competitors in the same industry in the United States and Europe.

However, for a company desiring to receive the Deming prize, this is not an acceptable attitude. We must not be concerned with comparative data with U. S. and European competitors. We must establish a goal of our own, which we can accept and be proud of. We must then take up the challenge which this goal provides.

And when it is time to submit your records for the Deming prize audit, be prepared to say proudly that your records have not been equalled anywhere in Japan, in the United States or in Europe.

(2) Developing attractive new products.

We used to equate "quality" with "no defectives." But today the emphasis is on "developing attractive new products."

We have established as part of our major policy goals, establishment of a "product planning system" and the creation of a "technology development system." Your cooperation will be very much appreciated, especially from those of you who are in marketing and in technology-related fields.

Upstream Control and Coordination Between Divisions

(1) Upstream control.

Twenty years ago when Toyota Motors received the Deming prize, I was a division manager in a machining works. I used to preach to my workers that "Quality must be built in during the manufacturing process," and "No matter how good it may be, inspection cannot create quality."

About five years later, a new thought emerged. That was to say that "Quality must be built in with design." We discovered that many problems which we faced in the factory were often created somewhere upstream, especially at the design stage. From that time on, we began to stress the importance of "upstream control."

Lately we have moved one step farther. We now insist on building in quality at the stages of planning and development.

(2) Interdivisional coordination.

Even before we started to use the term "upstream control," I had consistently emphasized the importance of interdivisional coordination.

In almost any company, important problems which must be solved are normally spread over several divisions. Therefore their managers must actively seek each other's opinion and come up with a joint solution.

We used to have slogans like: "Interdivisional problems are the responsibility of the division manager," and "Intersectional problems are the responsibility of the section chief." But as we look at these problems, about 80 percent of them can be solved very quickly if the preceding process improves its work. The work of the subsequent process can flow smoothly.

Therefore, today, I wish to ask you to give careful thought to one issue in your position as section chiefs. Please ask yourselves this question: "Is there anything we are doing in this section which can hamper the work of the subsequent process?" After you have thought about this issue, talk to one another. As you discuss these matters of common concern, most of the interdivisional and intersectional problems can be resolved.

Lately some of the technology-related divisions have been going around to factories, which are their subsequent process, and asking questions: "Please tell us what we have done this year which has not been up to par." After receiving responses from various plants, they compile a list of what they must do. I consider this one of the best examples of "going around to listen to latent complaints."

Most people would like to think that their own work is going along just fine. They would never feel the necessity of asking around to expose their own shortcomings. Conversely, if they hear complaints, their first reaction is to make an excuse, and seldom is there a concern expressed that they must take measures to prevent recurrence.

I hope the above is not your practice. When you receive a complaint, say "thank you" to the complainer. He has brought to your attention something which must be corrected. He has given you some seeds for improvement. This is the spirit with which we can promote interdivisional coordination.

After this, always keep in mind what measures you can take to help solve the problems. In some instances, it is entirely appropriate to say: "We plan to improve these items, but can we ask you to make some improvement on these other items?"

Interdivisional coordination is strengthened when you are able to improve in the way you handle things which affect other divisions. You can drink *sake* together and have an evening of fun with each other. But that alone cannot make a good system of coordination. I do not mean to discourage any of these social meetings. It is desirable if you can use these gatherings to smooth over human relations and create a better atmosphere. So there is definitely a place for such social gatherings.

QC-Type Approach

We have studied this many times, but just to make sure, let us review it once more.

(1) Market in (customer orientation).

We also say "customers first." Another favorite expression of ours is: "The next process is our customer." Application of this principle outside the company means to secure the satisfaction of our customers, and within the company it means to secure the satisfaction of the next process.

(2) Turn the cycle of PDCA steadily.

As we turn the control cycle of PDCA (plan, do, check, action), we also engage in a lot of related study activities, and they include the items reproduced below.

Some people may want to put each of the items listed below under a big heading and classify it as one of the major divisions. For the sake of clarity and simplicity, may I cite items one by one with a few words of explanation for each?

a. Stratification.

You are processing one specific product with two machines, Machine No. 1, and Machine No. 2. When you are studying the product's defective rate, do you separate the product into those produced by Machine No. 1 and Machine No. 2?

b. Setting priorities.

"I like to do this and I like to do that." You may want to do everything, but there is a limit to what you can do. Thus you must choose what is most important, and what is next in importance. You can set your priorities, and then do your work in the order of priority thus established.

In establishing countermeasures for defectives in the workplace, draw a Pareto chart, and start attacking the problems one by one from the largest one on the chart first. You can consider the Pareto chart a tool for setting your priorities.

c. Cause factor analysis.

What are the causes of chronic defect and sudden defect?

The simplest way of analyzing these cause factors is to use the cause-and-effect diagram (often called the fishbone diagram). Show this diagram to everyone present, and ask each of them to give his opinion on a plausible cause factor. You can determine statistically which cause factor is more pervasive than the rest. There are a number of statistical quality control methods which can be utilized for this purpose. If the matter cannot be settled statistically, you can try out one cause factor and then another. If this method is impractical to use, you can ask a person who is conversant with proper techniques to make a guess.

Once the cause factor is known, you can establish your countermeasure. In olden days, when defectives occurred, foremen gave admonitions such as "Be more diligent," which was followed by the workers' "We will." But they did not know what to look for, and they could not prevent recurrence. Today, we analyze cause factors and take action which leads to prevention of recurrence. Herein lies the importance of PDCA.

d. Process-oriented.

Do not worry about the results, but be concerned with the process. Observe how the workers work. If defectives are found, think carefully to see which part of your process has caused it. If you cannot reach your annual policy goals, think carefully to see if some of the methods of implementation have been faulty. In olden days, some people thought that by saying "Do your best" to the workers, they had discharged their obligations as supervisors. That method never worked in the past, and is not likely to work today.

e. Standardization (no backsliding, prevention of recurrence and lateral dissemination).

The word "standardization" has two meanings. The first meaning is found in the process leading to the creation of the "Japanese standards" and "international standards." We standardize size, weight, quality, strength and the like to make manufactured goods interchangeable. This meaning is also applicable when we say: "Let us standardize with the metric system."

In QC, we use this term differently. We establish technical standards and work standards. When we do our work in accordance with these standards and something does not turn out right, we amend the standards one after another. Therefore along with the word "standardization," we may say "no backsliding," "prevention of recurrence," "lateral dissemination" and "lateral development."

When we amend these standards to bring about improvement constantly, we create an accumulation of knowledge in technology for our company.

f. Upstream control.

When we investigate cause factors for something which has gone wrong, we may find difficulties arising from the process itself, but frequently the difficulties may come from the immediate or farther-up preceding processes.

You use a Pareto chart to analyze defectives found in a mass-produced item. One of the cause factors may well be that there was carelessness at the stage of either production preparation or design. In olden days, we never bothered to go upstream to investigate cause factors. But today it is almost a routine occurrence, and those upstream processes are beginning to be concerned with the effect they may have on the downstream processes also.

g. QC story.

Generally when the term "QC story" is used, most people view it as the order in which presentation of QC improvement projects is made. But it is more than that. It is also the order through which improvement activities are conducted. In other words, you can follow this order to engage in your improvement activities, and then follow the same order when you make your presentation.

A QC story generally includes the following categories. If you want to emphasize one of these categories, you can subdivide it, and give a more detailed explanation for that particular category.

1. Background (reasons for selecting this theme).
2. Investigation of the present condition.
3. Analysis.
4. Measures taken (trial run, implementation).
5. Confirming the results.
6. Standardization.
7. Remaining problems and how to proceed in the future.

Some people think that another category should be created and inserted between items 1 and 2. That category comes under the heading of "establishing goals." In most instances, reasons for selecting the theme include articulation of goals. Thus I do not favor including an additional item for "establishing goals."

When presentations are made, many presenters include a summary statement about the company and about the process. This is done either before or immediately after item 1 is presented.

h. Maintenance and improvement.

Most circles and foremen can now discover abnormalities and take measures quickly as part of their maintenance control activities. That is a definite plus. However, I am still not satisfied with one aspect of these activities. That is the inability of most QC participants to say "Something different must have happened in our process. What could that be?" while starting to analyze abnormalities.

The phrase does not really matter. I will accept it if they say: "Is there anything different from yesterday?" In any event, there is still lacking amongst them an idea that they must always be on the lookout for something which is different.

The problem is not confined to Toyoda Gosei. Many Japanese companies do not have this down pat. Here is an extreme case which occurred at a presentation meeting: "An abnormality has occurred and we are adopting it as our theme. We hope to solve this problem within three months." This does not help either the company or QC, but cases like that are found now and then.

From my point of view: "If workers do not understand, the fault lies with the method of teaching." These QC circle members were not at fault, but the problem lies with the way in which they were taught. As section chiefs, I want you people to remember this example and teach your subordinates accordingly.

i. Routine control and policy control.

Strictly speaking, routine control means that regardless of the existence of a policy, control must be extended to everything which is supposed to be done. If there are some issues which cannot be resolved, which are chronically troublesome, or if there is a request from customers for a faster delivery, and if these matters require six months or a year to resolve, then they must be placed on the annual policy. The term "policy control" refers to the manner in which annual policies are determined, how they are developed, how they are checked and what actions are to be taken.

Therefore routine control involves maintenance control activities while policy control must be concerned with improvement activities. However, when improvement takes only one or two months to complete, it is best to include such activities under routine control. We do not want to make the items in the annual policy become too balky.

j. Control item table.

In QC the term "control item" and "control point" are frequently used and may convey different meanings. My definitions are as follows: When we say "determining manufacturing quality with the rate of defectives at shipment inspection," the term "control item" refers to the manufacturing quality, and the term "control point" refers to the rate of defectives at shipment inspection.

Therefore a control item table is a table which assembles the control items of a certain job function and the control points. If the term "control point" is difficult to comprehend, substitute it with measures, yardsticks or evaluation measures.

To someone who is just beginning, I ask: "What graphs or source materials are you consulting?" I then show them how to differentiate between those providing information and those requiring action. When they assemble the latter, they can create their own control item table.

(3) Control through facts.

a. Dispersion control and control through data.

This is the basis of statistical quality control. Toyoda Gosei is a company which bases its main manufacturing on rubber and resins. It is not used to analyzing matters quantitatively such as by size or weight. But here we are engaged in TQC, and we must be prepared to observe everything quantitatively. There are many areas in which we can utilize statistical quality control.

This is an ideal opportunity for us to introduce the notions of dispersion and process capability in the company's QC activities; whereas, in the past we used only the number of defectives and percent defective as the evaluative criteria.

I knew about these things when I became president. But I did not emphasize these points to you. In setting priorities for our company, there were many other points which I wanted to stress. But the time has come for us to study these problems. May I ask your cooperation on this?

b. Observing the actual item at the actual location.

When you devise countermeasures against defectives, do not confine yourself to your office. Go to the place where those defectives occurred, and study the actual item. You can obtain far more information than if you remain in your office. Do not just follow the data given to you on your desk. At the actual location you can devise much better countermeasures.

c. Speaking truthfully (*honne*).

If the atmosphere is not conducive to speaking truthfully, saying what is really on one's own mind (*honne*), facts can be hidden.

For example, the "preventive maintenance man" and the "die exchange man" work independently, and seldom do they come under the scrutiny of their supervisors. Suppose there is trouble; no measure can be taken unless we know if the trouble occurred in spite of the fact that all standards were observed, or if it occurred because standards were not observed. The same can be said about those people who are sent out for temporary assignments, and for salesmen.

Why do I not say "Don't lie," and instead state "Say what you really think (*honne*)"? This is so because the nuance in the first phrase assumes that you "have a habit of lying." When you create that kind of feeling among workers, human relations can only get worse. I take the sting out of that saying by insisting on "creating an atmosphere conducive to speaking with *honne*" or "speaking with each other with *honne*."

(4) Respect for humanity.

a. Full participatory management.

When a section chief asks his subsection chiefs to come to a meeting, it is not enough for them to be present. It must be a meeting where everyone present speaks up, creating a feeling of full participation.

b. QC circle.

Section chiefs are in an excellent position to assist QC circles. You must tell QC circle leaders that you always ask your subordinates to speak up in meetings. If necessary, give these leaders a pointer or two about the way you make this happen.

One of the most common complaints we hear from many QC circles is that "Our superiors are not interested in our QC circle activities." I am sure no section chief in Toyoda Gosei falls into that category. But I still worry about full participation with respect to everyone speaking up. The other day I saw the results of a survey. In 1982, the rate of speaking up was 60 percent. It reached 80 percent in 1983. I want the rate to reach 100 percent by the end of this year. I hope you will consider this as one of our priorities. Our QC circle meeting usually lasts about an hour. If two out of 10 participants remain silent, it is an indication that these two are not really interested in participating in QC. These two could well be the ones who need to raise their consciousness about quality.

Some QC circle leaders may be prone to selecting themes which can later bring about a larger sum of money saved for the company. When such themes are selected they tend to be more technical and difficult to comprehend. Participants may not feel that they can participate meaningfully in discussion. You must be prepared to extend help to your QC circle leaders on the matter of selecting themes. This responsibility may fall on foremen rather than on the section chiefs. Be that as it may, you must give sufficient guidance to your foremen about this.

QC Techniques

I have no intention of explaining each of the QC techniques here. However, I want to make sure you know which techniques are important for you as section chief. Table 8–1 divides QC techniques into three categories and assigns priorities. Please consult the table, and if you find that you need additional knowledge on some category, please plan to acquire it as soon as possible.

The signs in the table signify the following:

(a) ◎ indicates that these items must be studied.

(b) ○ indicates that these items are to be implemented at the point when the companywide level of QC has been raised.

(c) △ indicates that all foremen whose job calls for control charts and process capabilities must study this particular item.

Group / QC techniques	Top management	Middle management	QC staff	Foreman	QC circle Leader	QC circle Member
Seven tools of QC (Pareto chart, cause and effect diagram, etc.)	◎	◎	◎	◎	◎	○
Simple SQC (Control charts, process capabilities, etc.)		◎	◎	△		
Difficult SQC (Experimental planning method and above)		□	◎			

Table 8-1: List of QC Techniques Which Must Be Studied

(d) □ signifies that "It is sufficient to be able to judge if these difficult QC techniques are to be used."

II. Questions and Answers

Question 1. What Concrete Steps Must One Take to Help Promote Interdivisional Coordination?

I wish to address my question on the issue of interdivisional coordination. In our factories, most of the problems are caused by the poor work of some of the preceding processes, such as the production engineering division or the technology division. However, no matter how loudly these factories complain, they are never listened to. How do you cope with situations like this?

Answer

In addition to what I mentioned earlier in this book about interdivisional coordination, please keep the following in mind.

In QC, we are guided by the principle of "market in" (or customer orientation). Within the company, this means that "the next process is our customer." We must always be concerned with customer satisfaction at the subsequent processes. The most important lesson for those people in the technology or engineering divisions is that they cannot slacken down on their work, lest they inconvenience the factories who are their subsequent processes.

At Toyoda Gosei, too, the technology division used to listen to complaints from factories reluctantly. But last year, the division started to go to the subsequent processes to solicit complaints. When this is done, those who normally would complain also begin to "organize their own thoughts in an effort to provide adequate information for the technology division for the latter to take appropriate action." Everyone benefits from this arrangement.

This is an aside. The other day, an American team came to observe, and they were very interested in this particular issue. They were seriously concerned with this matter and wanted to know how this type of coordination could be effectively transplanted and implemented in their own companies.

There is another important issue which we must not overlook. There used to be a time when I visited our plants that I always encountered problems similar to the one experienced by you. The Pareto chart for defectives clearly showed that the largest cause factor came from the preceding process, and the plants could not solve these problems on their own. Fearing that this could be used by the plants as an excuse for not doing anything, I ordered that any improvement which had to be done by the production engineering and technology divisions should be clearly stated. If there were some items for which Toyoda Gosei did not have its own technology, they were to be registered as "bottlenecked technology." I emphasized the fact that those problems which were not caused by preceding processes would have to be dealt with promptly by the process itself.

As this practice was spread, it coincided with the initiation of making the rounds to ask for complaints which the technology division so expertly handled. With these practices, our number of defectives decreased significantly.

Question 2. Can the United States Engage in Interdivisional Coordination?

In Chapter 1 of Part I, you said that those division managers who cannot practice coordination should go to work for an American company. But there are many American companies which are engaged in TQC today. When American companies practice TQC, can they effect this kind of interdivisional coordination?

Answer

Recently when an American TQC team came to Toyoda Gosei, this became one of the topics of our discussion.

It is a very difficult problem for most American companies, but some companies are working hard to promote it.

I gave them these words of encouragement: "If interdivisional coordination becomes a reality in the United States, its TQC activities will be materially strengthened. It is something to look forward to."

Question 3. Is Taking Measures Against Abnormalities Such an Important Issue?

In your talk on maintenance control activities, you stressed the importance of taking measures against abnormalities. You almost have a pathological dedication to taking measures against abnormalities.

Answer

As discussed earlier, as soon as a report of an abnormality is received, the supervisor must take prompt action. This cannot be delegated to QC circles. The supervisor must investigate why it has happened and devise countermeasures.

When the line is stopped because of abnormalities, the workers there have nothing else to do. In such a case, the supervisor may ask them to help. Help can also be secured from the staff or from the superior. But it is important for a supervisor to remember that he is the one who is responsible and he is the one who must take action promptly to correct abnormalities.

Question 4. How Do You Conduct Your Routine Control?

I have heard that Toyoda Gosei has done a lot for policy control for a number of years. How well are you progressing in your routine control?

Answer

As mentioned earlier, policy control tries to solve those problems which cannot be solved by normal routine activities. But the basis of its activities is still routine control. There are two types of routine control.

The first kind is to establish standards and let workers observe them. If abnormalities occur, along with the taking of emergency measures, standards are revised to prevent recurrence.

The second type is to engage in small improvement activities. If a problem requires six months or a year to solve, it must be included in policy control. Other improvement activities which are not major ones can be considered as part of routine control.

At Toyoda Gosei, we train our managers and supervisors in "maintenance activities" and "small improvement activities" and teach them how to implement them. Our top management is very interested in the adequacy of materials in checking the progress of these activities, and in the fact that managers and supervisors make use of these materials.

When I inspect adequacy of routine control by section chiefs in the workplace, I always ask the following question accompanied by some requests:

"Please show me your control item table."

"Please show me the materials on those items classified as the 'A' category in importance."

"There was an abnormality which was reported. Please tell me how you took care of it."

"To prevent its recurrence, which standards did you modify?"

Question 5. Will You Show Us How You Make a Control Item Table?

"Conceptually it is not too difficult to understand what a control item table is. But when we try to make one ourselves, it is not easy to do." This is a fairly frequent complaint. How do you teach these people?

Answer

Among all middle managers, section chiefs in the manufacturing processes will probably have the easiest task in compiling a table.

Go to some of these section chiefs and examine the materials they have to consult every day, or at least once every month. Examine also those items which must be included in the section chiefs' annual policies before they can be solved. Choose a section chief who is most enthusiastic about QC in the workplace, and send a QC staff member to work with this section chief in creating a table. After the staff member becomes thoroughly familiar with the section's work, he prepares a manual. The staff member can then take this manual along with some concrete examples to other section chiefs. There the staff member again makes the table for two or three section chiefs. In the process, he revises the manual to make it even easier to understand. In this fashion, the tables for all sections in a plant can be completed. After this is done, the same procedure can be applied to administrative and technology-related divisions.

An actual example from a section chief in a workplace is given in Table 8–2.

Question 6. What Can One Do in a Meeting Where Themes Discussed Are Not Part of One's Own Responsibility?

Mr. Nemoto, you emphasize that everyone must speak up in a meeting. But at meetings, we often encounter themes which are unfamiliar to us, for which we have no direct experience or about which we have no jurisdiction. When that happens, it is difficult for us to speak up. How can we prepare ourselves to be in such meetings?

Answer

We can be mentally prepared for this type of meeting by observing the following:

1. When you listen to the presentation, assume a positive attitude of "Let me learn something I have not known before." If there is some-

Category		Quality		Cost
One which is included in annual policy		X		
Degree of importance		A	B	
Control item		Quality of goods at delivery	Quality of process	
Control point		No. of claims by recipients of goods	No. of defectives within the process	
Control material		Graph of No. of claims per month	Graph of No. of defectives per month (per process)	
Date of checking		5th of every month	5th of every month	
Measures against abnormalities	Standards for taking measures (when)	When one incident occurs	When it goes over the control level	
	Method of taking measures (how)	Investigation of cause factors Counter-measures Prevention of recurrence	Reviewing the process Improvement measures	
Note				

Table 8-2: Control Item Table—Example of Section Chief in a Workplace

thing you do not know or understand, open your question with these words: "I am sorry to show my ignorance, but can you enlighten me on this point?" That is all it takes to get the information you need. It is a wonderful opportunity for you to expand your intellectual horizon, and it can lead to varied approaches.

2. In solving a theme, the presenter may not have listed its steps accurately. You can formulate your question by following the QC story.

The methods he has used in his analysis may be faulty, or his analysis and measures taken may not jibe with each other. You may have no direct experience concerning the theme under discussion, but you can still question if the method of confirming results has been correctly used. You can also ask about the techniques and order used in implementing improvement activities. While asking these questions, you can enhance your own ability toward improvement!

3. An observer often has keener eyes in discerning advantages and disadvantages in the Japanese game of *go*. This is also true with improvement plans. Those who are responsible have been concerned with the same themes for so long that they may lose their objectivity, while people who are not directly connected can devise better alternatives. So you can make your suggestion by saying: "I hope you do not mind having an outsider's uninformed view."

Once in a while, good suggestions are given through this process. That is why I insist on everyone speaking up in a meeting. Without it, many of these valuable suggestions may never see the light of day.

Question 7. Can You Truthfully Admit Your Own Mistakes?

In some companies where they have a strict system of "rewards and punishments," employees are not accustomed to telling the truth about their own or colleague's mistakes. Do you use the term "rewards and punishments" in your company?

Answer

No, I do not. When that phrase is used, the accent always seems to fall on "punishments." It creates a feeling of "we better avoid mistakes," for fear of being punished. A company cannot survive without a spirit of taking up the challenge of the new.

In olden days, we used to hear these words spoken: "I have been able to discharge my responsibilities until retirement without committing major errors." This does not foster the spirit of challenging the new.

165

I am convinced that no employee will deliberately do harm to his company. If he has done his best and has been careful, but still a mistake has occurred, can he really be blamed and punished? He is the same person who was hired after rigorous examinations and interviews. Since his first day with the company, he has been trained by others and has learned the standards given to him. Can you punish him because he has made a mistake? I cannot. His mistake is not of his own making, but the responsibility must be shared equally by the one who hired him, by the ones who have trained him and by those who have given him the standards.

I stress "investigating the causes" over "determining the responsibility." In the context in which it is used, the word responsibility seems to be followed by the word punishment. When we know who is responsible for a certain mistake, punishment follows.

In our criminal codes, there is a right to remain silent. In a company, if someone is likely to be judged for a mistake committed, his colleagues are likely to remain silent. When this happens, the true cause will never be known. We end up taking wrong countermeasures.

If a mistake committed is not deliberate, I usually say: "Tell me the truth please. You will not be held responsible. It is more important for us to be able to prevent recurrence." Once we know the truth, we can effectively prevent recurrence. When the company can prevent recurrence, its effectiveness increases.

In a company, if you want to assess the guilt or non-guilt of your employee and determine the punishment to be meted out like a court, the process may take many years to complete. The company itself will end up the biggest loser.

Question 8. How Different Is Your Method of Teaching About Work and About Sports?

In Part I you said that you never scolded anyone. In the current TQC promotion movement, have you kept up with your own principle of not scolding? In sports, coaches shout at their trainees. Are companies and sports so different in their approach?

Answer

Business and sports cannot be compared in this manner. In sports the body must master all the motions through training, and this is in addition to the knowledge acquired through the brain. If one is concerned with acquiring special skills, he must be prepared to endure pain.

In imparting knowledge, yelling is not necessary. But the exercises which are designed to let the body master special skills are a continuation of pain. The coach yells and at the same time encourages. How to strike back at a serve in volleyball is a taxing exercise. Players repeat it with sweat and tears. They are exhausted and shouted at. But in front of the coach no one can say that they want to quit. Hard as it may be, the exercise continues.

In business, the body cannot be pushed to the limit of its endurance. When that happens, the company cannot expect to have sustained work from its employees. In a company, the work is not supervised. Whether his superior observes it or not, an employee must do the assigned work in the manner predetermined for him.

You may wonder why so much of a company's work is not observed. In an assembly conveyor for a car, a squad leader can seldom observe what the workers on the other side are doing. But without supervision, these workers must master the skills to do the work in accordance with the standards set for them. There is no need to shout at them.

As you can see, the work of a company and sports are fundamentally different.

9

Strengthening the Design Division: A Case Study of Top Decision Making

---

I. Decision Making at the Top

"That's Good—Let's Do It" Formula

One of the important decisions I have made since becoming president of Toyoda Gosei without consulting others was that of "strengthening our design division." Many people commented afterwards: "That was a decisive action. As a specialist of TQC, I am sure you had many forecasting materials at your disposal before you made that decision. You didn't say 'That's good, let's do it,' and suddenly decided to do it. Did you?"

Every time a question like that is raised, I answer in the following manner:

The decision I made in strengthening the design division was indeed based on the "That's good, let's do it" formula. I could have given instructions to my staff to prepare forecasting materials on the future

169

needs of the design division. But I was certain that the materials prepared by them would not be satisfactory. Even if they could forecast some future needs, there would be so many uncertain factors included in their estimates, and nothing they could imagine would be any better than what a common sense approach could provide. Timing was far more important to me than to wait for the completion of these rather unreliable forecasting materials.

If there is time, it is good to have all the forecasting materials on hand to make a decision. But if the most crucial element of timing is lost, the decision reached would not have much meaning. If a top administrator always insists on having his staff prepare materials before making a decision, efficiency of the staff would suffer considerably.

Four Ways of Top Decision Making

My own process of decision making may be divided into the following four categories:

(1) "That's good, let's do it," while hardly investigating the matter. Assuming that the Japan Union of Scientists and Engineers (JUSE) asks me to become a member of its Deming prize committee, I will say yes immediately. I do not need to have my staff prepare a report forecasting the merits and demerits of accepting this assignment.

(2) After giving careful thought to the implication for the future from different angles, the top executive makes his decision—"That's good, let's do it."

This is the area in which top executives spend most of their time. With regard to the strengthening of the design division, I thought about the matter carefully, but without the benefit of forecasting materials. Not wanting to lose the timing, I decided to go ahead with it.

So far I have dwelled on forecasting materials and timing, but there is another factor which must not be overlooked. That is the issue of "maintaining corporate secrets." If the staff is ordered to prepare forecasting materials, they must be told why the materials are needed. Therefore, the greater the need to maintain secrecy, the harder it is to assemble materials.

In cases like this, existence of forecasting materials aside, a decision must be made. In the end this process may appear to be similar to the one discussed earlier, that of "That's good, let's do it."

This form of decision making is based on the executive's own experience and feel or sense (*kan*). It cannot be considered a scientific approach, but is still frequently used.

(3) A special staff assembles all the necessary information to make a forecast. That is analyzed and coordinated, the president mulls over all the alternatives and finally makes the decision.

Decisions affecting product planning fall mostly in this category. Also included in this category are matters related to the building of a computer center, such as where to build it and how many stories it must have. It is true that the "Let's do it" sign is given under this category also. But it is quite different from the "Let's do it" sign under category 2. It is not a great decision. It is often a decision closely following the recommendations made by the staff.

(4) When the special staff assembled information, they could come up with only one answer. When this fact is presented to the president, no room is left for him to pass judgment, and he decides accordingly.

Let us say that you are making a profit projection for the year, and the special staff comes up with this evaluation: "Changes mandated by the tax reform law become applicable this year. Thus the following changes must be factored in for this year's calculation." Obviously you are not going to have another plan, and your decision must be based on the plan as submitted by your special staff.

A profit projection is normally a matter reserved for the top management. But in this case, there is no room left for choosing alternatives.

The above four categories describe my views on top management decision making. The general public, however, usually identifies only categories 2 and 3 as belonging to top decision making.

TQC and Top Decision Making

As we ponder on the relationship between TQC and top decision making, we realize that some of the decisions made under category 2 may not be expressed in the form of a QC story, even though the president may go through his thinking process in a TQC manner. If we want to force a point, it can still be considered a TQC decision, because it is determined by an executive who has used a TQC approach based on his rich experiences in TQC. But sometimes, it is easier not to say that this type of decision is made on the basis of TQC. It is easier for the public to understand it this way. I also know that some top executives do not wish to explain their decisions with a QC story, and because of that have become detractors of TQC.

However, once the president makes a decision, its development and promotion must be conducted by all the divisions in the company affected by that decision. From that point on, TQC's approach becomes indispensable.

The policy I established to "strengthen the design division" has been implemented through companywide cooperation, and is accomplishing what it has set out to do. By promoting it as part of our companywide TQC activities, I need not oversee it in minute detail, and still everything has gone smoothly. Of course, on matters which require closer scrutiny, we have turned the wheel of the PDCA circle many times.

Matters relating to category 2 may be expressed differently in the following manner. The president decides on "what to do," but all the affected divisions determine "how to do it concretely" in a cooperative TQC fashion.

In the case of category 3, TQC can be counted on to make a great contribution. All the information which may be needed is assembled and analyzed. It makes it easier for the president to make a decision. For staff members, this represents the most challenging type of work. They can also utilize QC-type approaches and techniques for category 3-type decision making.

II. Decision to Strengthen the Design Division

Soon after I became president of Toyoda Gosei, I decided to strengthen our design division in the manner described under category 2 above. I like QC so much that my approach has always been completely and unequivocably QC. But in this particular instance, there were no materials which could be used in "investigating and analyzing" as prescribed in the QC story. Furthermore, there was no forecasting of design needs, and we could not ask some outside research organizations to prepare one as they do for economic conditions. It was not possible for any reliable forecast to be obtained.

May I now elaborate on what went through my mind.

Trend Toward Variety

Toyoda Gosei is a comprehensive manufacturer of auto parts. As automobiles become multifarious, there tends to be a larger demand for higher-priced cars, along with individualized and fashionable designs.

Our company makes car handles. In a certain type of car, previously only two types of handles were required. However, in the future we expect to design five or even 10 types of handles for it. Customers' demands necessitate it, and our design division must be strengthened.

172

Customer-Based Design Division

While the need for design is increasing, most companies are afraid to increase their employees in this field, and are asking outside organizations for support.

People in the design divisions are a different breed who have special talents. When they are in short supply, a company cannot quickly fill vacancies. There is also a fear that today's short-supply may turn into tomorrow's oversupply, and no company is willing to take a chance on this.

Be that as it may, I do not consider the current shortage of design people a temporary phenomenon. We will be needing more and not less. This is especially so, when we consider that cars are becoming more individualized and fashion-oriented.

Contributing Toward Lead-Time Reduction and Cost Planning

Once Toyoda Gosei's design division is strengthened, it can serve its customers—i. e., carmakers—more effectively. It can participate in a carmaker's planning and design stage preparations and help shorten the lead time.

At the planning stage, Toyoda Gosei can consider designs which meet the customer's cost plan. In short, it can be part of the customer's value engineering from a very early stage.

Previously, carmakers drafted their blueprints, gave a copy of each to two suppliers asking them to submit competitive bids and then selected one to become the supplier for the parts.

However, such a practice can no longer meet the need to shorten lead time to survive in the fiercely competitive marketplace. Nor can such a practice meet the goal established by the customer's value engineering. Carmakers will eventually be forced to seek out suppliers which have the design capability and can participate in the carmakers' work from the stage of planning. This is one of the reasons for my wanting to strengthen our design division.

From Hardware to Software

Viewed from a long-term perspective, such as a span of 10 or 20 years, I can see a clear trend away from our emphasis on hardware to an emphasis on software. The terms hardware and software have meanings beyond their conventional use in computers.

In computer language, the term software means to create a system or a program, but here I like to give a wider meaning to the term by including the following: how things look, how they feel to the touch and how well they are designed individualistically and fashionably.

It was only a few years ago when words like "upscaling," "individualizing" and "making it fashionable" were first used to describe a desirable car. I think this trend will continue to be strengthened year after year.

Five Times More Designers in Five Years

For the reasons cited above, I decided to strengthen our design division. As to its scope, no one could come up with an answer. So after giving the matter some thought, I decided to expand the number of designers five times in five years.

Five times the present level means to have 60 designers in five years. I have had no material to consult, and the goal was established by me unilaterally. That was another of my typical "That's good, let's do it" decisions. Normally companies may establish goals such as 50 percent more in five years, or double the quota in five years. But seldom do people establish a goal of five times in five years.

III. Priority Measures Taken to Strengthen the Design Division

Establishing a New Design School Within the Company

On October 1982 when I became president of Toyoda Gosei, there were 12 designers in our employ. I wanted to increase that number by five times to 60 in five years. However, there had not been a large number of design specialists seeking employment with Toyoda Gosei. Our normal quota was one a year at most. If we continued this practice, it would take another 50 years before we could reach the goal of 60. We had to find some alternative solutions.

What came to my mind was establishment of an in-house design school, selecting as its students our employees who have the ability and potential, and giving them an education equivalent to that of a junior college.

Scouting for a First-Rate Director

My first concern was who should become the leader of our in-house school. Fortunately there was one Mr. Mamoru Yaegashi, who was once head of the design division of Toyota Motors, and until recently was Associate Director of CALTY Design Research, Inc. in the United States. He became the chief instructor of the school and oversaw its entire curriculum.

We named the school the Yaegashi School of Design. We did this in part to announce to others that something unusual was taking place at Toyoda Gosei, and also in part to show our confidence in Mr. Yaegashi, wanting him to be fully responsible and in charge of the school.

Selecting the First Class

Among our employees there should be some who have talents in painting and sculpturing and who have not been recognized for these talents. I estimated that there should be at least one out of 100, so I asked our employees to apply on their own without receiving any further recommendations.

At the same time, I asked heads of different divisions in our workplaces to recommend at a ratio of one out of every 100. Thus if the self-recommendation and superior's recommendation overlapped, it would signify to us that the person had the talent we were looking for and would make our process of selection much easier.

As expected there were about 50 applicants, and we put them through the following three stages of our selection process.

First evaluation—Examining works submitted. The applicants' paintings and sculptures were exhibited and examined.

Second evaluation—Creativity and ability to make things. We actually let them draw and create things.

Third evaluation—Willingness, personality and overall evaluation. This was designed to determine if they were interested in making designing their lifetime work. As to their personality, there were some letters of recommendation from their superiors. We still had to make certain that they could stand on their own as designers, and discussed the matter openly.

Finally we selected 14 employees for our first class. There were two female workers among them.

IV. Characteristics of the Yaegashi School of Design

Full-Time Education

The 14 people were transferred to the design section and received full-time education. The goal was set to provide the equivalent of a junior college education which was to be completed in two years.

Characteristic as a Group of Varied Talents

These people were selected from different divisions of the company and had varied experiences. Among those included in the group were: a design engineer for metal molds, a line worker of metal molds, a forklift operator and a member of the QC staff.

Unlike a group who has just graduated from school, there was always someone who could utilize his experience to contribute to the class progress. For example, if the school needed a cutter for completing its clay model, someone who had experience in toolmaking would go to his previous workplace to make it. In this way everyone participated. They had a special sense of belonging to the first class, and they exuded confidence and vitality.

Training in the Making of Clay Models

Generally when we use the term "designer," we refer to those people who have graduated from a department of design from college. They are classified as professional employees. Modelers, on the other hand, are regarded as someone closer to experienced workers in the workplace. Therefore, all companies treat the two functions as separate ones, and no one is expected to do both types of work. In an extreme case, in some companies, designers are considered office workers, while modelers are considered line workers.

In our design school, we decided to include the making of clay models as part of our training. In our company there was no differentiation between office and line workers, and there was no resistance to the introduction of this training. When a designer learns to form a clay model, he can transfer his own design directly into a clay model to express his artistic ideas. This has helped the company in shortening its lead time.

Extending the Areas Between Planning and Designing

When we plan and design a new product, we normally go through the following steps: product planning—designing—transferring to a blueprint. Actually we go through these three steps back and forth doing the same thing over and over again before we complete the design. Nowadays, when we must introduce an attractive new product very quickly, we cannot follow these three steps in our traditional way. Something must be done to quicken the steps. Our solution is to let the three steps move in a parallel manner as much as possible.

Thus a designer may not just draw a picture. He can go to the preceding step or to the subsequent step. And to accommodate this practice, our educational program has been accordingly modified.

Practicing to Make Things with One's Own Hands

In a normal school education there is a serious restriction on materials and equipment, and seldom do students have a chance to make things on their own. In the case of our design school's first class, they were given this chance. By the end of their first year, this class was organized into groups of two to three persons, with each group engaging in all areas of new product planning and design. They did everything conceivable, including the drafting of blueprints, making trial runs and evaluating their own products.

There was a group which created a new type boat, and put it on a test run in a company swimming pool. The group gave its own evaluation and presented the results in a meeting. This is something no junior college freshman can do.

V. Accomplishments and Future Plans of the Yaegashi Design School

Activities of Its Graduates

The first class of 14, after completing two years of training, are now at the front line of company activities. At their graduation, they all gave reports before me, and I was confident that they had acquired the abilities which I had expected them to acquire.

This is the first training program of its kind in Japan. I know there are many areas in which modification and improvement are required. These can be incorporated into our next plan. I expect the school to become even more enriched in its curriculum step by step.

A New Design Center

A design center, three stories tall, with 1,000 square meters (1,196 square yards) of space is being built over a three-year period. The center has processing machines and precision measuring instruments. With the addition of these new facilities, we are also planning to expand our training program.

For the Second Class and Thereafter

Our initial plan of increasing the design division's employees to 60 people is on course. One notable change is taking place recently. We are now seeing an increase in new graduates with design majors wanting to enter our design division. They are graduates of design schools, and it means that our own Yaegashi school of design no longer has to start with the very basic courses. To respond to this change, our design school may gradually be transformed to have a curriculum similar to that of a Master's degree course.

For example, if a design school graduate has had no experience in making clay models, the Yaegashi school can give him special training in clay-model making for six months.

I made the decision to strengthen the design division in 1982. Three years later, in the process of the Deming prize audit, it was judged to be a good decision. I hope five or 10 years from now, people will still say: "Mr. Nemoto made a good, forward-looking decision at that time."

VI. Questions and Answers

Question 1. Was the Strengthening of the Design Division One of the Most Important Aspects of Your Deming Prize Audit?

In 1985, when Toyoda Gosei was audited for the Deming application prize, you chose the design division as the one which "the company wishes to present most actively (under the so-called Schedule A)." Was this your own idea?

Answer

Yes, it was my idea, and it came about due to the following reasons:

1. No other company had ever emphasized its design division while applying for the Deming application prize. I wanted to show the unusual quality of our company in this field.

2. In TQC we are now emphasizing more and more long-term strategy. Toyoda Gosei wanted the committee to know of its long-term commitment by examining the strengthening of the design division which happened to be a brain-child of its president.

We also wanted to emphasize how well TQC had functioned from the stage of decision making to the stage of its implementation.

3. All companies stress their human resources development. When we speak of human resources development, we normally emphasize education. I wanted to point out that there was another step before providing education which was equally important. This step could be expressed in the following terms: "To discern the special quality in each individual," and "For a special project, seek out a person with the ability

to handle it." People have their own special attributes. We must find them and expand their ability. I wanted to show that through our actual examples.

4. At most companies, the design division always takes a back seat when it comes to TQC. In contrast, we have had companywide cooperation in promoting the establishment of the Yaegashi school and in operating it. Everything has been promoted according to QC's approach, and I was confident that the committee would fully approve of the steps we took in this regard when auditing us for the prize.

Question 2. What Are the Factors in the Success of Your Policy of Strengthening the Design Division?

The success of Toyoda Gosei's policy of strengthening its design division is obviously due to Mr. Nemoto's timely decision. Additionally, am I correct in assuming that your concurrent active promotion of TQC has materially aided in the design division's success?

Answer

Yes, indeed. If we had not had our TQC, things would not have moved as smoothly as they did. There are several reasons:

1. The policy put forward by the president was accurately translated into concrete terms and accepted as implementation items under TQC.

2. While the training program was progressing, the wheel of PDCA was turned around many, many times.

3. When we needed personnel for the division, various divisions unstintingly sent some of their most capable people.

4. There was a companywide commitment to the cause. Many former superiors of the members of the first class often came to see them and offered words of encouragement and support.

10

Groupwide
Total Quality Control:
Helping Affiliates
Establish TQC

I. Necessity for a Groupwide Movement in TQC

Purpose of Groupwide TQC

Toyoda Gosei received the 1985 Deming application prize. With this, the company's special attributes (*taishitsu*) were substantially strengthened as compared to the time prior to receiving the prize.

But we could not rest on our past laurels. If we were to survive in a continuously changing world and respond to the difficult situation ahead of us, we could not remain content and ignore a few remaining problems. Our new resolve was to stand on higher ground and adopt a policy of strengthening the special attributes of the entire group, including our suppliers.

This is what we found, after we surveyed the conditions surrounding us:

Among our suppliers, there are some large materials makers who are in many ways leaders in their own industries. There are also some affiliated plants, who are small in scale, and whose performance is not always up to par. We have no special problems with the former in terms of quality and date of delivery when we receive from them shipments of resins, rubber and other materials. Our relations with them have been good, including the areas of exchange of information and joint development. We have very little to worry about dealing with these large suppliers.

On the other hand, the same cannot be said with regard to some of the small affiliated companies. It is true that they have studied QC along with Toyoda Gosei for a number of years. But there is a significant difference between their level of attainment and that of ours. Lately, it has become apparent that more and more problems are caused by the affiliated plants. It suggests clearly that a wide gap does exist between us.

As part of our new approach, I plan to promote QC vigorously among these affiliated plants. The emphasis will be placed on the following two points:

1. We plan to raise the level of QC at these affiliated plants to the level of Toyoda Gosei.

We have done well with quality assurance and cost improvement. We want to have lateral dissemination in these areas to our affiliated plants in accordance with their size. Shortly after the Deming prize audit ended, many of Toyoda Gosei's own plants indicated that they wanted to help our affiliated plants study QC. When I heard this, I knew that I could count on them to start promoting a groupwide TQC program.

2. We hope to raise the level of coordination with our affiliated plants to the level of coordination existing between our own divisions.

In promoting TQC, I always emphasize that "the next process is our customer," and "Are you doing something which can be troublesome for the next process? Go over there to ask if there are any latent complaints." I want to extend these principles to our affiliated plants also.

We must consider our affiliated plants our next processes. We must try to find out our own shortcomings which have made work at these affiliated plants difficult. We hope they will tell us about our shortcomings directly, even without our going to their plants to solicit their complaints. In this way, we may be able to promote improvement at a much faster pace.

To these affiliated plants, I plan to say: "Please don't hesitate to complain to us about what we are doing wrong and give us any suggestions you may have. When you tell us what we are not aware of, you provide us with seeds for improvement. If we can act on your suggestions to bring about improvement, it strengthens our company's special attributes. Therefore, supply us with more of your complaints and suggestions. The more you provide, the greater is your contribution to Toyoda Gosei!" At the same time, when I make a round of our divisions, I ask this question: "What complaints have you received, and what improvement actions have you taken?"

When we speak of cooperation with our affiliated companies, we often think of teaching them how to do things and deny ourselves the wisdom they can provide for our own enlightenment. Hereafter, I want to place an equal weight on the second point.

Another Purpose in Helping Our Affiliates

The two points cited above characterize the program we have in mind for our affiliated plants. However, I am hoping to obtain an additional side benefit. We are going to have many of our middle management people serving as instructors for these affiliated plants. It is my hope that through this act of teaching, they, themselves, will become strengthened in their own abilities.

When I evaluate our employees, I use the following four categories.

◎ Excellent understanding of QC. This person can go to another workplace and lead them effectively.

○ Adequate understanding of QC, but not at the level of guiding others in another workplace.

△ Somewhat deficient in the understanding of QC.

X Absolutely no comprehension.

For example, after we complete the study of the Toyota production system along with some practice sessions, I evaluate each participant to see if he has attained the level of ○ . My hope is that anyone who has attained the level of ○ can move to the level of ◎ in the next round of training, and can become an instructor elsewhere. Between ◎ and ○ , the gap is quite significant. To be able to teach others requires a substantially higher degree of sophistication.

We can, of course, apply this procedure not just for the Toyota production system, but also for QC.

II. Concrete Steps Taken to Guide Affiliated Plants

Cooperation Urged of Top Management

I continue to tell top executives of our 90 affiliated plants as follows:

"Toyoda Gosei plans to have a seven percent increase in sales annually under its long-term plan. We hope to attain this goal no matter how difficult the surrounding conditions may be. Any of you who wish to grow with us, please raise your hands. I want to pledge to you that we shall grow together.

"To those of you who have raised your hands, I want you to know that we expect you to maintain a similar level of attainment in QC as we do at Toyoda Gosei. I plan to promote even more vigorously our cooperation in mastering the art of QC. May I count on your help?"

If these top executives will agree to strengthen their companies essentially on their own, then you have it made. That desire to do something must always be considered the first ingredient to success.

How to Provide QC Instruction for Affiliates

In practical terms, there are three steps we can follow:

1. There is a cooperative association which is sponsored by our 90 affiliates. This association holds nine separate organizational activities. We shall assist these activities vigorously and disseminate through them thoroughly the QC approach and QC techniques.

2. We shall provide QC training for the affiliates' top management, middle management, supervisors and QC circle leaders separately. These separate study group sessions are intended to raise the consciousness of all employees of these affiliated plants towards QC.

3. We shall provide individualized training for some of the companies which are especially important to Toyoda Gosei.

As to the methods we employ in providing individualized training, I plan to ask each of the companies under training to register with us their priority tasks. We also ask these companies to identify problems which are important to them, and show to us their concerns and worries about the future. As they think about these issues, the problems can become clearly defined.

At the same time, Toyoda Gosei will point out to these affiliated plants, what are important issues from its own perspective, with the criterion being how effectively the services of the affiliated plant may be utilized. The list which an affiliate has made, and another list which Toyoda Gosei has made, are scrutinized together and compared. From

184

these two lists five most important tasks are selected. For each priority item which is selected, we determine its target value, showing the date when we expect the goal or solution to be reached, say within a year or two. At this time, we also determine control points (evaluation measures) and supporting materials.

For example, in dealing with quality, we may set up targets for defectives within the process, defectives at the time of shipment and the number of defectives delivered to the customer. If Toyoda Gosei has a similar process, the targets set for an affiliate must be close to the targets which Toyoda Gosei maintains. If there is no similar process, what Toyoda Gosei expects of its affiliated plant becomes the target set for the latter.

As to the instructional items, we will of course want to be consulted on what measures the affiliate plans to take in reaching the goals set for priority tasks. For each of the implementation items, Toyoda Gosei must also be prepared to state clearly which aspects require special attention. For example, at the stage of production preparation, we must spell out what kind of foolproofing (the so-called *pokayoke*) is expected of them. Whatever can be spelled out must be done so from the outset, and this includes our expectations about revitalizing the affiliate's QC circles.

Persons in Charge of Instruction

Now who should be the one to provide these technical and other instructions? I plan to establish a section in charge of providing instruction to affiliated companies within the division of purchasing. This section is to be responsible for guiding the affiliated plants in matters relating to the overall plans and common items. However, I hope the system can be made flexible enough, so we can solve matters case by case in accordance with the facts presented to us. True learning of QC comes from observing and experiencing. I hope this case-by-case approach can be utilized for that purpose. When problems occur in our affiliated plants, I expect our section chiefs to be there to assist, and also serve concurrently as instructors in QC.

Up until now, we have been satisfied when defectives are no longer produced. We say: "Great, we don't have any defectives." This attitude must change. Get into the habit of confirming the fact by insisting that the affiliate submit its schedule. You may ask: "To prevent recurrence, we want to see how you standardize your process. Can we have a report on it soon?"

III. Toyoda Gosei Prize in Quality Control (The TG Prize)

In giving individualized guidance to our affiliates, I have often felt some form of incentive, such as a prize might be in order. My current thinking is that we establish a Toyoda Gosei prize in quality control for this purpose. In this chapter, we shall refer to this prize as the TG prize.

However, when we establish such a prize, people may feel that it is a mini-version of the Deming prize, and smaller companies may be too embarrassed to apply for it. So a special consideration is necessary. After giving much thought to this issue, I have come up with the following outline.

An Outline of the TG Prize in Quality Control

1. In our evaluation, the weight given to the company's regular performance is 90 percent. The weight given to President Nemoto's visit occupies the remaining 10 percent.

2. The regular performance grade is to be assigned by the division manager or section chief (normally from the purchasing division or from Toyoda Gosei's plant) who has been responsible for instructing the affiliate in QC.

3. The regular performance grade is generally determined by observing how well the matters agreed upon between Toyoda Gosei and the affiliate as priority items are progressing, and how closely the goals have been attained.

4. The evaluation by President Nemoto will be based primarily on presentations given by company officials supported by several sheets of materials. He plans to include as one of his questions: "How well have you complained to Toyoda Gosei and thus contributed to the latter's improvement effort?" There will also be a simple, wandering-around inspection of the plant.

5. President Nemoto's visit will be conducted at the rate of one company a month, starting in January 1987. Toyoda Gosei plans to apply for the Japan Quality Control Medal, for which preparation must begin in 1990. Therefore the granting of the TG prize must be concluded by the end of 1989.

IV. Questions and Answers

Question 1. Is the Groupwide TQC Going to Be Your Biggest Selling Point Toward the Japan Quality Control Medal?

Immediately after receiving the Deming application prize, Toyoda Gosei declared that it planned to challenge the Japan Quality Control Medal in five years. Is there another company which has done that? Do you plan to make your groupwide TQC a selling point at that time?

Answer

As you know, when companies are audited for the Deming prize, there is a meeting between the evaluating committee and the top management. I understand that at that meeting, some executives will say that they plan to mount a challenge toward the Japan Quality Control Medal. So we are not alone in this. There are several points we want to present when we are audited for the Japan Quality Control Medal, but certainly the groupwide TQC is going to be one of them.

Question 2. In Your Groupwide TQC, Are You Prepared to Help Fill the Personnel Needs of Your Affiliates?

Mr. Nemoto, at your annual New Year's message, you indicated to the presidents of your affiliated companies that in promoting your groupwide TQC, you were prepared to help them fill their personnel needs. What do you mean by this?

Answer

There are some companies which receive our guidance in TQC and can reach the targets established under their priority tasks without any further assistance from us. That, of course, is fine with us. But there are other companies which require far more assistance than that. Conditions prevailing in such companies may not allow us to wait. In such instances, we consider active support from Toyoda Gosei which may include the sending of our own personnel.

We may send our people to these companies for two years, and longer if necessary. We also accept employees from our affiliates for training at Toyoda Gosei, and there is no limit to the number of employees we can receive. In fact we are prepared to accept as many as requested.

Question 3. What Are Your Responsibilities to Your Suppliers as Their Preceding Process and Subsequent Process?

At the same New Year's party and in the same speech you spoke to your suppliers as follows: "To our suppliers, I want to mention that Toyoda Gosei is a preceding process and a subsequent process to you. May we be of assistance to you in your QC activities, as we discharge our obligations as your preceding process and subsequent process?" What do you mean by discharging your obligations as a preceding process and a subsequent process, all at the same time?

Answer

The responsibility of a preceding process is not to inconvenience the subsequent process, because the latter is its customer. It is a fundamental concept in TQC. If the subsequent process (affiliated plants) no longer complain to us, we must be prepared to go to them and actively seek their latent complaints. For example, we may go to them and ask: "As you study the drawings and blueprints we send you, do you see anything which is difficult to read or easily misunderstood?"

Our obligations as a subsequent process are as follows: If we find some defectives from a supplier, it is not enough to say that "we found some defectives." We must provide them with appropriate information, so they can take measures against recurrence. We can go a step farther by confirming that they have standardized their preventive measures against recurrence. This can lead to the strengthening of the supplier's ability to perform. Our company must be dedicated to performing this responsibility as a subsequent process for our suppliers.

Question 4. Is It Easy for Your Affiliate to Complain to You?

Mr. Nemoto, you seem to expect your affiliates to keep on complaining to you, so there will be many improvement suggestions for you under the groupwide TQC movement. Generally speaking, affiliates do not dare complain to their parent company, and employees of the parent company do not like to receive complaints. Can you realistically expect that you can create an atmosphere under which complaints can be aired freely?

Answer

The attitude of Toyoda Gosei becomes the crucial factor here. When we receive complaints, we must be prepared to say: "Thank you," and really mean it. We must be able to listen to our suppliers with an open mind. And when we complete our improvement, we must report the results to the one who has reported that matter to us. If no improvement is effected, we must explain to the same party why it has not been possible to make the correction.

One of the important functions of the president is to see which divisions of his company are receptive to the airing of complaints and which ones are not.

I also want to emphasize the following to our affiliates: "Please complain to us more frequently. When you do so, you are contributing to the strengthening of our special attributes."

With this kind of endeavor from both sides, we hope to create a climate which is second to none in Japan in its ability to allow free exchange of opinions.

Question 5. Do You Have Some Affiliates Who Reject Your TQC Guidance?

You are offering a lot to your affiliates. But by chance do you have some affiliates who reject your offer?

Answer

Some companies may be willing to participate in study seminars sponsored by the nine cooperative associations or in QC seminars provided for different job categories. But they may be reluctant to state that they want to receive our individualized guidance because they want to apply for the TG prize. There are companies whose degree of dependency on Toyoda Gosei is fairly small, and the amount of their sales may not be large. I know there are many reasons which can prevent them from participating, and there is no desire on my part to force participation on them.

For Toyoda Gosei too, if all 90 companies decide to apply for the TG prize in 1987, we will not be able to handle it.

An ideal situation for us is to be able to give the prize sequentially to the affiliate which is most important to us, followed by the one which is next in importance.

Question 6. What Plans Do You Have for Those Affiliates Whose Degree of Dependence on Toyoda Gosei Is Not Significant?

Assume there is a company whose degree of dependence on Toyoda Gosei is only 10 percent, but it comes to you and says: "We want to

189

apply for the TG prize and study QC. Can you provide your indivi-
dualized guidance for us?" How do you respond?

Answer

A company that eager is a very promising one. I want to extend
our assistance, and while doing so, I wish to reevaluate the use of that
company's services in the future. When a firm is that enthusiastic, I do
not think it takes much to guide that company. And yet, if this approach
proves inefficient, we can always withdraw from our assistance agreement at that time.

Question 7. There Are Some People Who Say: "You Can-
not Make Money Off TQC." What Is Your
Reaction to This?

I wish to pose this question as the president of one of your affiliates.
I know my parent company is right about TQC and I want to pursue
it. But here is a cacophony from another quarter: "You cannot make
money off TQC!" Shall I disregard this cacophony?

Answer

To produce profit, companies must engage in various things. TQC
is a tool to make our management more efficient. And unlike many other
tools, it is a very useful one. If managers are sold on TQC and use this
tool effectively, they can bring about the strengthening of their company's special attributes, along with an increase in profit. However,
one cannot expect his company's profit to rise by merely saying that
"We are engaged in TQC."

As you promote TQC, defectives which have always been one of
your major problems will decline, and cost reduction will take another
step forward. Just with that much, your profit picture will be substantially improved. A more important issue is the strengthening of your
company's special attributes. You become a company fully trusted by
your parent company. There is a promise of continuous growth along
with that of your parent company.

Question 8. Do You Expect Your Dealers to Participate
in Your Groupwide TQC?

I understand that you use the services of dealers in some areas.
Do you plan to include these dealers in your groupwide TQC?

Answer

Our dealers engage in part of our marketing activities. This is a good time to redefine and clarify our respective marketing responsibilities, and make coordination of activities between dealers and other divisions of the company an even better one.

I expect our marketing headquarters to become the main organ in promoting these activities. As to the question of making the dealers eligible for the TG prize, we must investigate the matter further.

Question 9. When an Affiliate Receives the TG Prize, Can It Expect Orders from Toyoda Gosei to Increase?

I understand that by promoting TQC groupwide, affiliated plants and Toyoda Gosei become strengthened in their special corporate attributes. Will there be a danger in the perception that while receipt of the TG prize may earn an increase in orders from Toyoda Gosei, failure in obtaining the prize may result in a decrease? This perception may force your affiliates to apply for the prize unnecessarily. At the same time, there may be complaints that the receipt of the prize has made no difference in the amount of orders received.

Answer

Just because an affiliated plant receives the prize does not mean that Toyoda Gosei's order to that plant will increase the next month. The 25-product list of Toyoda Gosei includes handles and hoses, and each of these products grows at a different rate. Therefore, the receiving of the TG prize does not lead to an increase in our order.

However, Toyoda Gosei is setting as one of its long-term goals an increase of seven percent in annual sales. Those affilated plants which want to grow with us are invited to participate in our groupwide TQC as a means of growing together.

In the long run, there is bound to be some differences in the amount of work to be performed by those which have received the TG prize and those which have not, because of differences in their special corporate attributes.

Question 10. How Do You Deal with the Unevenness in the Level of Your Affiliated Plants?

If you guide those plants which desire your assistance in QC, their level will rise, and the better ones become even better—and the overall unevenness will become even more pronounced. Don't you worry about this?

Answer

Unevenness of this type does exist, and the gap between those which have received the prize and those which have not can be very significant. But all we have to say is that those which have attained the higher level must go up even farther.

There is no need to tell those who are on the upper levels: "Please remain still for a while," so the remainder can catch up. When some good plants become even better, the overall performance record of the 90 affiliated companies also rises. We do not have to ask good ones to remain static.

Question 11. How Do You Promote Coordination Between Affiliated Plants?

In a groupwide TQC program, it is of course important to make the ability of each company better. But at the same time, we must strengthen coordination between affiliated companies. In your talk you did not touch on this subject. Do you have any specific plans?

Answer

As I mentioned in the section on how to provide QC instruction for our affiliates, I plan to utilize the activities of nine separate groups sponsored by the cooperative association of our 90 affiliates. These nine groups can become the vehicles in promoting coordination.

These nine groups hold study sessions. We have been sending people in charge of purchasing to these sessions to give advice when appropriate. From time to time, division managers and section chiefs from Toyoda Gosei, who are in related fields, are also asked to participate in these sessions. For example, our production engineering division manager and section chief of mold design may attend a study session on metal molds, and explain to the group our improvement examples. At the same time, they can listen to candid opinions and suggestions from the affiliates.

As we plan for coordination among the affiliates, we plan to strengthen the activities described above. Toyoda Gosei is prepared to give additional assistance to these activities.

Question 12. When You Let Your Own Section Chiefs Become Instructors of QC, Do You Determine Ahead of Time Which Plants Are to Be So Instructed?

Mr. Nemoto, you spoke of having all of your section chiefs from various Toyoda Gosei plants serve concurrently as instructors for affiliated plants. You want the affiliated plants to learn and experience QC through actual practice and work. But there may not be consistency in this type of instruction. Do you worry about it?

Answer

Yes, I have thought about this. One of the plans I now have is to divide our section chiefs according to their areas of specialization, such as rubber, resins, caps and clasps, and metal. We then assign those who are most closely connected to the subject to an affiliated plant which needs their services. "Company A needs Mr. X and Mr. Y," and "Company B needs Mr. Z" and the like. I believe continuity can be maintained through this system.

Question 13. Your System May Impose Too Much Burden on Your Section Chiefs. Will It Not?

Section chiefs in your factories must administer their own workplaces. Now you are asking them to help teach QC to your affiliates. Will this additional burden adversely affect their own work?

Answer

We have tried this system out in some plants, and the results have been very good so far. However, we also have unevenness among our own section chiefs. Some of them may be just beginning to become acquainted with their jobs. In that case, we try not to overburden them. Their teaching assignments can be given to chiefs of the quality control section, inspection section and engineering works.

Question 14. Do We Adopt Only Those Priority Tasks in Our Annual Policies?

As your affiliates, some of us are establishing our own annual policies. Is it permissible to include in our annual policies some items which are not coordinated with Toyoda Gosei?

Answer

Reduction of industrial accidents and traffic safety are subjects not likely to be included in the coordinated priority items. But if an affiliated plant of ours wishes to include one or both of these items in its annual policy, that is of course fine with us. However, we can have problems if coordinated priority items are excluded from that company's annual policy.

Question 15. What Are the Central Themes in Priority Tasks?

Many of your affiliated plants are processing manufacturers. They are not likely to adopt themes such as product planning or technical development as their priority tasks. What will be their priority items?

Answer

I think quality assurance and cost control are the subjects which will remain in the center. In the case of quality assurance, emphasis will be on production preparation, and on control of initial mass production and mass production. In some affiliated plants, they assume only partial responsibility for production preparation. In such a case, only the matter of direct concern to that affiliate can be placed in the central position.

As for cost, labor cost and equipment cost have always claimed the largest share. An emphasis may be placed on the number of workers withdrawn from the work force, as determined under the Toyota production system. Lately efficiency resulting from the use of computers has also become an important issue, which may also be included in the affiliate's consideration.

Question 16. When You Have Five Priority Tasks, You May Have Assigned Too Many. What Is Your Opinion?

You mentioned that Toyoda Gosei and affiliated companies will get together to narrow down their coordinated priority items to five. But to a smaller company, five can still be too much of a burden. Doesn't that happen?

Answer

There are 90 affiliated companies. Amongst them are some very small plants which are responsible for simple manufacturing. In cases such as these, our requirement may be only two or three priority items. There is no magic about the number "five."

Question 17. How Do You Guide QC Circle Activities in Your Affiliates?

From your talks, it appears that you place a great deal of emphasis on guiding affiliates' QC activities to help them solve priority tasks. Don't you think it is just as important to activate and raise the level of their QC circle activities? Operating QC circles voluntarily and autonomously may not be an easy task in small companies. How do you help them overcome this problem?

Answer

Most affiliated plants participate in the QC circle presentation meeting sponsored by Toyoda Gosei as part of its observance of the quality month. They exchange opinions and make presentations, and they can judge where their own QC circles stand in relation to those in other companies.

If they find that "activating and raising the level of QC circles" must become one of their priority items, I am confident that they will pick that as one of their goals. If they ask us at Toyoda Gosei to guide and provide assistance, of course we shall be happy to do so.

If defectives within the process are caused by workers, then there is no question that the QC circle is the most effective means of handling the problem, and the affiliate must be so advised.

Question 18. When You Provide Guidance, Don't You Also Create Problems for Your Affiliates?

If you determine your TQC guidance plan and plan for auditing for the TG prize at the convenience of Toyoda Gosei, you may create problems for your affiliates. What thought do you have on this specific issue?

Answer

You have expressed two concerns in your question. One is about scheduling. We are both busy, so we must consult each other before determining our schedule. We cannot set the date unilaterally and go to an affiliate and lose our temper when its president is not available.

The second issue deals with the question of whether the contents of our guidance are helpful to the affiliate or not. We establish priority items first through mutual consultation before entering into this guidance phase. So ideally there is nothing involved which is unnecessary. At times there may be some items included which are really not needed. Then there are other items which the affiliate may consider spurious at the time implemented, only to discover later that these items have been indispensable in its growth. Utility of the guidance we extend may vary. In the final analysis, if it is not useful to the affiliate, then the entire effort may be in vain.

There is a tendency in guiding and auditing for the activities to assume momentum of their own, escalating their demands unnecessarily. They may demand preparation of supporting materials unnecessarily and cause unnecessary spending of time. So we must ask ourselves another question: "Are we escalating our demands unnecessarily?"

Question 19. Can the TG Prize Be Judged Through the Regular Performance Grade?

Can you really judge a program through its regular performance grade only?

Answer

In the case of the Deming application prize, experts from the evaluation committee came to the company for a day, and completed their audit within that time. In the case of our affiliated plants, they are mostly processing manufacturers and can be considered an extension of our own production lines.

We observe their quality at all times. We also confirm their delivery dates on a regular basis. We go back and forth between our lines and their plants frequently, and if we want to assign a regular performance grade, it can be easily done. We have also registered our agreed-upon priority tasks, and everyone pays attention to them. This makes it much easier to assign a regular performance grade.

Question 20. Do You Need Supporting Documents for the TG Prize?

When you are assigning a regular performance grade, you probably do not need a document explaining actual conditions. However, when you visit in your capacity as Toyoda Gosei's president, do you need such a document for your audit?

Answer

Priority tasks have already been narrowed down to a very few, and it is best not to impose any extra work on our affiliates. If a document explaining actual conditions is desired, for each of the priority items a QC story may be written on a sheet of paper double the letter size (or 16½ × 11¾ inches).

I explained in some detail about the QC story in Chapter 8 of Part II. The candidate for the TG prize can explain the progression of its improvement by enumerating its activities from "reasons for selection (or background)" through "how to move forward into the future." If they want to add something to this, they can submit the actual supporting materials they are using.

My policy is not to create unnecessary work, and if they spend too much time preparing these materials, that fact can actually go against them.

Question 21. How Many Years Are Required to Prepare for the TG Prize?

I understand that you will begin examining candidates for the TG prize starting in January 1987. That does not give your affiliates much time. A year is hardly enough to prepare for the prize.

Answer

Among some of our affiliates are those with a substantially high level of QC attainment. Those affiliates which handle our safety parts began their study of QC at the same time Toyoda Gosei did. Their ability to "foolproof" is almost as good as ours. In fact, if they are not at the same level as we are, we cannot entrust our safety parts to them.

Then there are yet other affiliates which were audited along with Toyoda Gosei when we were a candidate for the Deming prize. They did so to provide supporting evidence for our attainment.

To those companies which are presently at a relatively high level, if we simply intensify our guidance, they can reach the level of the TG prize within a year. By starting to grant the TG prize in January 1987, we hope to promote our groupwide TQC at an accelerated speed.

On the other hand, there are affiliates which handle a series of products such as resin and plastics parts which are not related to safety. It takes anywhere from two to three years to confirm their quality and delivery dates. For these affiliates, we want a deliberate approach, and let them take their time to study and do their utmost in meeting our common goals.

Question 22. At the Time of Your Audit, Do You Plan to Audit Subcontractors of Your Affiliate?

When you were audited for the Deming prize, there was an advisory audit of your suppliers. In the case of your own TG prize, do you intend to examine your affiliate's subcontractors?

Answer

When our affiliate plans to apply for the TG prize, we want them from the outset to identify problems and establish goals. If at that point problems related to subcontractors are judged to be one of the priority tasks, we must initiate a program of guidance which includes the subcontractors, and then later confirm the fact that indeed the levels of the subcontractors have risen.

For example, if it is found that one-half of the problems related to quality have been caused by subcontractors, that affiliate company must make their supplier problem one of its priority tasks. Our own audit of that company, of course, must take this into consideration.

Question 23. Will Some of the Affiliates Be Rejected for the TG Prize After Mr. Nemoto's Visit?

I understand that the final phase of the audit is Mr. Nemoto's visit. Is there any possibility of an affiliate being rejected at this point?

Answer

I plan to make my visit an occasion which marks the conclusion of the splendid work our affiliate has done. Assuming that all the priority tasks which were registered before have been accomplished, and the process reaching that goal has received a "good" grade, then all I have to do is go over there and say: "Thank you so much for your good work. You have now reached the level of Toyoda Gosei. Let us work together always." I shall then make a round of their plant. I doubt anyone will fail this final inspection.

Assuming that an affiliate has received good marks in most areas, but a few unsatisfactory marks in the remaining areas, if they can reach the satisfactory mark within three months for the latter, I do not mind conducting my "final" inspection tour at that juncture. We can declare that they pass the audit as of three months hence.

Question 24. How Important Is It to Know QC Approach and Techniques for the TG Prize?

I assume that some of your affiliates are small-scale operations, engaging only in simple manufacturing work. They may have only two or three priority tasks. Do you still expect them to know the QC approach and techniques?

Answer

When we are engaged in individualized instruction, we are dealing with those priority tasks we have agreed upon. In a narrow sense, as long as these tasks are solved as planned, the program has met its goal. But when its process is not based on the QC approach, or if the use of QC techniques is wrong, they may encounter other difficult problems in the future. It is best if everyone masters QC. Do not be satisfied with the present level of accomplishment. If the affiliated plant wants to raise its level in the future, QC becomes an indispensable tool. Therefore, top executives must seize this opportunity to let everyone study QC and solidify the foundation.

There are a number of ways in which QC can be promoted. For example, our affiliate may adopt its priority tasks as goals for its QC activities. At the same time, in order to get its line workers to become interested in QC, various QC circle activities may be revitalized.

Table 10–1 indicates how QC may be learned by all employees, from the top to line workers.

The signs in the table signify the following:

(a) ◎ indicates that these items are required. The number on the shoulder indicates the order in which that specific item must be learned. 1-2

(b) ◎ sign appears under "QC staff." The two numbers on the shoulder mean that the staff may be the second person to acquire the skills, if the president is the first one to do so.

(c) ☐ signifies that "It is sufficient to be able to judge when these difficult QC techniques are to be used."

(d) △ indicates that all foremen whose job calls for control charts and process capabilities must study this particular item.

(e) ○ indicates that these are to be taken into consideration at

QC approach and techniques \ Group	Top management	Middle management	QC staff	Foreman	General (QC circle) Circle leader	Member
QC approach	◎[1]	◎[2]	◎[1-2]	◎[3]	◎[4]	○[5]
QC techniques — Seven tools of QC (Especially Pareto chart, cause and effect diagram)	◎[1]	◎[2]	◎[1-2]	◎[3]	◎[4]	○[5]
Simple SQC (Control charts, process capabilities)		◎[2]	◎[1]	△[3]		
Difficult SQC (Experimental planning method and above)		□[2]	◎[1]			

Table 10-1: Order of Study

the point when the companywide level of QC has been substantially raised.

Question 25. Do You Have a Prize for Smaller Affiliates?

The Deming prize has a special category for small- and medium-size enterprises. Do you have prizes for smaller companies?

Answer

Most of our affiliates are small in size with only about 100 employees. Thus the TG prize itself is for small and medium-size enterprises.

We want these affiliates to become self-reliant and dependable in the areas of quality, delivery and cost. We want to discuss with them the acceptable levels for both of us.

Our affiliates are different from one another. Among those affiliates who mold our resin-based products, some start from the stage of designing molds, and yet others may start from the stage of procuring equipment. There are still others who do mass production on molds provided by us. Each of our affiliates has its own special functions and responsibilities, and therefore its priority tasks also differ from one another.

The TG prize has only one name, but items to be examined under the prize differ according to types of company. To take an extreme example, assuming that an affiliate mass-producing plastics parts receives the TG prize, it does not follow that they can begin designing metal molds. I want to drive this point home to everyone who plans to apply for the prize.

Question 26. How Do You Handle Affiliates' QC Education by Job Categories?

If your affiliates plan to establish QC education for their middle management and foreman classes on their own, it would be an enormous burden for them. I assume that you plan to have a joint education program for them. Which division in Toyoda Gosei will be handling this?

Answer

In QC education, we normally begin with group instruction for separate job categories. Our plan for our affiliates will be established by our purchasing division. As for its instructors, as much as possible, we shall have our own division managers and section chiefs serve in that capacity. For the top level people's QC education, I plan to serve as instructor in some of the more important sessions.

Question 27. Does Mr. Nemoto Plan to Serve as Instructor for Presidents of Affiliated Plants?

To promote QC at the affiliated plants, their presidents must become thoroughly educated in QC. If these education sessions are handled by section chiefs of Toyoda Gosei, it may create some weighty problems. Mr. Nemoto, do you plan to be an instructor yourself?

Answer

Yes, I am thinking of having a group meeting for the presidents. In QC, we are keenly aware of people's motivation. In a groupwide TQC like the present one, we need more than ever the commitment of all of its participants.

Some sessions may be handled by our plant managers and section chiefs. These sessions include a review session on QC, dealing with matters such as routine measures against defectives. If there is a need to effect a change in the thinking of our affiliates' presidents toward QC, then I want to conduct some follow-up sessions.

Question 28. How Do You Plan to Educate the Second Generation of Owner-Managers for Your Affiliates?

Like Toyoda Gosei, our company has a number of affiliates which are small in scale with about 100 employees each. In many of these affiliates, the management is about to be turned over from their founders to the second generation. Does Toyoda Gosei have any specific plan to educate these second-generation owner-managers, on whose shoulders the future of these affiliates may well depend?

Answer

In some of our affiliates which were established shortly after the Second World War, the generational change is also about to take place. In places like these, one of the best ways of educating the second generation of owner-managers is to make them responsible for QC promotion. There are many instances in which this approach has been successful.

If the prospective owner-manager is still very young, let him become the affiliate's co-director of the TQC secretariat, and let him serve as a liaison officer for the entire company. He can also be sent to Toyoda Gosei for a year or two, and experience TQC through his daily contact with us. He will learn how closely our work and TQC are tied together.

Question 29. Is It Wise for a Small-Scale Affiliate to Engage in Policy Control?

When an affiliate has only 50 to 100 employees, there is not enough staff personnel available to engage in policy control. How do you react to this situation?

Answer

When a company is that small and where there is no staff to speak of, it can certainly not be expected to observe the form of policy control as we do at Toyoda Gosei. Now let us think in terms of what is the minimum requirement in this situation. As discussed earlier, these small companies can start with one simple question: "What is the most important problem this company must solve?" Everyone studies it, and decides on solving it. This is the first step toward policy control. If after your discussion, you determine that your priority task is "too many defectives within the process," you can then set out to solve it. Everyone can now join in discussing where to place the target, and how to reach (implementation item) that target. Then everyone goes on to promote the program.

In the process of its promotion, if another priority task is found, add it to the list and follow the same procedure.

Top management must not sit back after helping to decide a target. A shout of "do your best" can sound rather hollow. If needed, top management must be prepared to contribute ideas, or money, or both. It must be ready to listen to the progress of the project every six months or so. This is what I call top hearing, about which a detailed discussion can be found in Part I.

So far, we have not used the term "policy control," but the foundation for policy control is there. At the next stage of this company's activities, all the priority tasks can be brought into the open, from which three or four may be selected to form the next year's annual policy. In a small company, all discussion sessions are attended by company directors. And this makes it easier for the program to move on and develop naturally.

When conditions like the above develop, we can say that policy control already exists.

Question 30. Does a Small Affiliate Need to Establish Its Own TQC Promotion Office?

In a company which has so few staff members in its administrative divisions, if it establishes a TQC office, the best which can be expected is one person in that office. Is there a need to establish such an office?

Answer

Toyoda Gosei with its 5,000 employees has only six persons in its TQC promotion office. If a company has only 100 or so employees, there is no need to exert itself by creating a TQC office. That task can be given to an administrative division or section which has a companywide responsibility.

However, to coordinate and discuss TQC, I suggest that a TQC promotion committee be created. If an existing committee is to be given this responsibility, let it put TQC on its agenda first. And then after a certain interval, stop the TQC part and allow the committee's normal discussion to proceed. It often happens that if TQC is combined with another committee, its agenda can be left to the very last. If it is combined with a production-related committee which is overly concerned with the present problem, for the week or for the month, time will pass—and when the allocated time comes, someone will say: "Let's wait until next week to discuss our TQC promotion." And this can happen again the following week also.

The head of this promotion committee must be the president, vice-president or an executive managing director who has real power in the company. If a second generation manager is already close to this rank, he may be given the title of vice-chairman, but in fact entrusted with full responsibility for promoting TQC.

To complete the organization, select someone who is most capable of coordination from the staff division to serve in the TQC secretariat. He then becomes assistant to the chairman of this committee.

11

What Executives Can Expect from QC Circles

I. My Involvement with QC

QC Circle at Toyota

I became an instructor for QC circles in 1964, when I was a division manager of the machining division at the Motomachi plant of Toyota Motors. The company promoted QC vigorously, and was preparing to be audited for the Deming application prize in 1965. Dr. Kaoru Ishikawa, the noted authority on QC, suggested to us that we should start QC circles within the Toyota group.

At first we had a modest goal of teaching QC techniques to the foreman class. We held monthly presentation meetings by section to give improvement examples. It did not take long for these foremen to master such techniques as investigating and improving process capabilities, and discovering and taking measures against abnormalities through the use of a control chart. In fact, we had the pleasant surprise of having too many volunteers who wanted to give presentations during the 1985 Deming prize audit. The initial aim of having our foremen master QC techniques was thus fulfilled.

From 1965 to 1970, I was division manager of the purchasing control division. One of my responsibilities was to serve as QC instructor for our affiliated plants. I created a system of evaluating QC circle's improvement examples. This system utilized a series of checklists. The details for these checklists are given in Chapter 5 of Part I.

Around that time, the foreman class at Toyota became active promoters of QC. They were pleased with what they learned about QC, knowing that QC was helpful in establishing measures against defectives, and they wanted to teach QC to their squad leaders. Thus many subgroups and mini-circles were created for this purpose.

However, in 1969 safety became a major issue for carmakers as the recall campaign system was established by law. If due to our own manufacturing errors we had to recall thousands of cars for inspection and repair, it would create an enormous financial drain for the company. We had to devise some means of raising the consciousness of workers toward quality.

Changes in the Goal of QC Circles

Around this time, in many workplaces, the object of QC training moved down one notch from the foreman class to the level of squad leaders. "Why not lower this one notch farther to the level of line workers?" was our thinking then. By letting our line workers organize QC circles, we could raise their consciousness toward quality.

Some plants were quite advanced in this regard and already had some QC circles organized along these lines. They already had many squad leaders who were highly motivated toward quality. There was a movement to disseminate their knowledge laterally to spread QC to the entire company.

The primary goal of QC circles at Toyota was significantly modified. It was no longer going to be merely for study sessions for the benefit of the foreman class in acquiring skills in QC techniques. It was to become a means for enhancing and maintaining workers' consciousness toward quality.

Toyota had a creative suggestion system which was instituted 15 years before QC circles were officially introduced. This suggestion system was also transformed into a medium through which workers' consciousness toward quality was to be raised.

Toyota and my present company, Toyoda Gosei, are prime examples of companies where work is always people-centered. Line workers are in the front line of our manufacturing activities and can determine how well our cars are built. Their consciousness toward quality makes a big difference. To maintain this consciousness at a high level is a never-ending task for the company. Naturally, we have high expectations for our QC circles.

II. Differences Between QC Circle Activities and Managerial Functions

Proper Functions of Foremen and Line Workers

Generally those maintenance and improvement activities in which the foremen in the workplace take charge are their proper functions. Even if they seek help from some of their front line workers, these activities still properly belong to the functions of the foremen. Even when all the subordinates of a foreman are involved in one of these activities, and these subordinates all belong to QC circles, these activities belong with the foreman's sphere of proper functions and not with QC circle activities.

The proper functions of line workers are to observe the standards given to them and to do their work. Most of their work consists of repetitious manufacturing—and, day in and day out, they must do the same work for an entire year. It is difficult to promote a consciousness for quality under these circumstances.

These workers must be asked to get together, to think together and discuss together, to search for better ways of doing things and finding ways of reducing defects. In this way they can enhance their quality consciousness. When people can get together to engage in convivial conversations, good results can multiply. Allowing the workers to have a convivial place to meet and discuss problems is one of the aims of QC circle activities.

The Japanese people do not wish to be alone. They want a sense of belonging and to be in a group. QC circle activities take advantage of this Japanese predisposition.

As for a theme for discussion at its initial meeting, my favorite is "How to improve our work in our workplace." A theme like "Let us observe work standards correctly" is not only uninteresting, but also impossible to use as the theme for discussion. Acceptable themes include reduction of defectives and cost reduction.

Enhancing Workers' Quality Consciousness

In QC circle activities, how much money the company has been able to save is not as important as how well the circles have been able to enhance the workers' quality consciousness. Once their quality consciousness is enhanced, they need not be told to "observe work standards," because they can do so naturally, and the overall quality level of the company will rise substantially.

Basic ideas behind QC circle activities, according to the *General Principles of the QC Circle* (prepared by the QC Circle Headquarters and published by the Japanese Union of Scientists and Engineers), are as follows [in the English version published by JUSE]:

1. Contribute to the improvement and development of the enterprise.
2. Respect humanity and build a worthwhile-to-live-in, happy and bright workshop.
3. Exercise human capabilities fully, and eventually draw out infinite possibilities.

However, in our company, we have changed the order of these basic ideas as follows which seems to fit us better.

(1) Enhancement of consciousness, enhancement of employee morale and creating a lively workplace.
(2) Enhancement of human capabilities (proper techniques and management techniques).
(3) Results of improvement.

All three of these ideas are to be combined to contribute toward the development of the company.

III. Diversity of QC Circle Activities and Measures to Deal with This Phenomenon

The basic form of the QC circle which the Toyota group has today was shaped in the late 1960s. Today we still follow closely the format of the QC circles organized around 1969 when Toyota Motors people met a couple of times each month to discuss their improvement activities.

Since that time the form of the QC circle has become varied, as many Japanese companies started organizing their own QC circles. There are QC Circle Conferences and even a QC Circle Cruising Seminar. When presentations are given at these and other meetings, and when the results are published almost simultaneously, confusion is bound to occur. The worst cause for confusion seems to come when proper managerial functions are included in QC circle activities.

QC circle activities have always respected voluntarism. When managerial functions are interjected into them, it forces QC to become something hierarchical, with commands given by the superior to QC participants. When this happens, the original purpose of QC is negated. Of course, when we speak of voluntarism, we do not mean to engage in a complete hands-off policy. Management can always extend assistance, but at the same time respect the circle's voluntarism. More on this subject later.

Categorizing QC Circles

How significant is the degree of voluntarism and autonomy? Does a particular circle consist of members from the same workplace? Using these criteria, I categorized QC circles and related activities and came up with Table 11–1. The table includes those circles which initially began their activities under other names, such as "small group activities," and the like.

The A group in the table represents the standard type QC circle as practiced in various workplaces in the Toyota group. Names other than QC circle are used now and then by our administrative and technology divisions to designate similar improvement activities.

In service industries, there are often only a few people working under a manager. No matter what name they may employ, their activities are bound to include managerial functions. Some of them, therefore, cannot be differentiated between B and C as contained in the table.

Some people do not like the term QC circle, and prefer to name their group "XYZ team." But this phrase can easily be confused with some project teams (such as G in the table) where people from different workplaces assemble. My advice is to stick with the name QC circle.

Let me say a few words about the table. At Toyoda Gosei, QC circle activities center around workplaces. Thus those in Category A and those designated B' in Category B are all called QC circles. (B) is called group activities and is differentiated from QC circle activities. I shall explain this further, but meeting time must be given to (A) and (B') without which their circle activities cannot function smoothly.

The above are typical activities within the Toyota group. Some companies may call D and F QC circle activities also. Each of these companies must make an effort to identify them appropriately and clarify their objectives as well.

At regional QC conferences or at cruise seminar presentations, these differentiations must be clearly stated to avoid confusion.

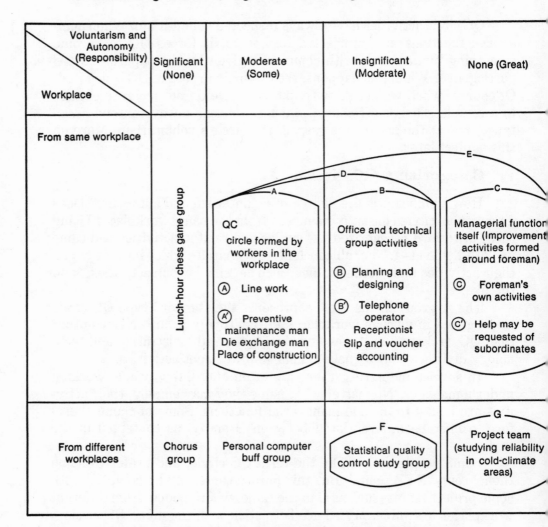

Table 11-1: Categories of Small Group Activities Which Are Similar to QC Circles

IV. Measures for Increased Assistance to QC Circle Activities

Companywide Activities to Help QC

1. Defining the position of the QC circle in the company and clarifying its objectives.

2. Establishing an organization to promote QC, and a QC secretariat.

3. Establishing a guideline for organizing circles, and providing assistance in actual organization (for each circle, the optimum number is between five and seven).

4. Educating superiors.

Have you seen a company where QC circle leaders know a lot more about QC than their foreman? If this happens, it does not work. Often we hear a complaint saying that their foremen and section chiefs are not interested in QC. This usually comes about because the company has neglected to train QC circle participants' superiors first from the top down.

5. Showing a guideline for selecting QC circle leaders.

Initially a squad leader may be appointed as the QC circle leader, and in a year or two let one of the line workers assume the position. A guideline like this will be quite suitable.

6. Providing QC education and training for leaders.

7. Establishing a guideline for meeting time. For example, two hours each month, on what day of the week, etc.

8. Holding meetings for sponsors and supporters.

9. Planning and implementing companywide QC conference or presentation meetings.

10. Educating and training QC circle members.

Steps a Superior in the Workplace Can Take to Help QC

1. Taking concrete steps in helping to organize the QC circle.

2. Helping to select the QC circle leader.

3. Helping to select the theme.

During the initial phase of the QC circle activities, show the circle several alternative themes and let the circle choose its own.

4. Helping to solve problems arising from promoting a theme.

Listen to the circle's report carefully and observe if everything is conducted step-by-step in accordance with the QC story. Be sure to call in the leader and speak to him on a one-to-one basis. If you go directly to a circle meeting, members may not feel free to speak up.

5. Helping to enhance the ability of leaders to preside over QC circles.

Do the meetings allow participants to speak up freely? Ask the leader about this, and if he is not able to create an atmosphere for it, give him some pointers on how to do it.

6. Helping in assembling and summarizing improvement examples

211

Hold several rehearsal sessions before the circle makes a presentation. This will train the members not only in the manner of presentation but also in the QC way of thinking. So take active steps toward holding several rehearsals.

V. Questions and Answers

Question 1. Can You Always Say That the Primary Goal of QC Circles Is Creation of a Lively Workplace?

Mr. Nemoto, you seem to insist that the primary objective of QC circles is to create a lively workplace accompanied by willingness to work and higher employee morale. In companies where they have had several years of experience, don't you think they can have as their primary goal, "results of improvement"?

Answer

There was a presentation meeting at a certain company. The results of improvement as presented were impressive, but there was no evidence suggesting that everyone participated in these activities. When I inquired about this, I discovered that the project was completed by the foreman with the assistance of two of his subordinates. The circle members knew nothing of the project until the rehearsal time.

I am, of course, for improvement projects which can bring these results. But, in this particular instance, the foreman was merely performing his proper job functions. He should not have equated this with the activities of QC circles.

Here is another story from a circle consisting only of female workers in a large company. They made a superb presentation dealing with measures adopted to combat defectives. One cannot fault it either from the standpoint of proper techniques or from QC. But I felt uneasy about it because of their exceptionally high level of attainment. "Could the project be conducted by a foreman and then presented as a report of the circle?" I asked.

The answer was a pleasant surprise: "This circle was formed four years ago by these same female workers. There has been no change in its membership. Without having a new person to train, the level of its members has risen substantially. When this circle makes a report within the company, all of its members come to the dais to field questions, and no one hesitates about answering. Yes, the level of this presentation is exceptional, and your question only confirms it. It is based on their own work, and we are very proud of them."

It is a good thing to see circles engage in improvement activities, raise their own abilities and then tackle more and more difficult themes. But here are some words of caution. If you go to a presentation meeting and encounter this kind of high level performance, don't be discouraged. Nor should you insist that all your circles attain the same level of accomplishment.

In a company which has just started QC circles, never say: "Pick a theme which will bring big results." Nor is the following statement advisable in another context: "We shall be having our third anniversary of QC circle activities. Don't you think it is about time that we have a theme with greater results?"

This is so because in a company with three years of experience in QC, those superiors and members of the QC secretariat may have attained a higher level of understanding about QC than during the first year; but at the lower end of the hierarchy, many QC circles still have to cope with the problems of having new members, changes in members and changes in their leaders. The example of the female workers, just cited, is an exception and not a rule.

You may want to raise the level of your QC circle activities, but when you start saying that a theme with better results must be selected, you may create more problems than intended. It is not always easy to find a theme which can produce greater results, but even when one is found, the theme selected is so difficult that it becomes difficult for everyone to speak up. This is one of the surest ways of leaving new members behind, denying them an opportunity to grow with their QC circles.

When a circle brings out some results but cannot create a lively workplace, it is not worthy of the name of a QC circle. If you are only interested in results, then ask your foremen to engage in their proper job functions. They can have a few people helping them, giving their opinions and participating in investigation and analysis, but these are not QC circle activities.

I insist on making a lively workplace my top priority in QC circle activities, because I want to emphasize these things I have just said.

Question 2. Can You Rely Only on QC Circle Activities to Bring About a Lively Workplace?

Mr. Nemoto, you say that the primary objective of your QC circle activities is to raise the level of loyalty and willingness to work among your line workers by creating for them a lively workplace. Do you think this can be accomplished by relying only on QC circle activities?

Answer

When I think of the objectives we have for QC circles, the most important objective is found in "raising the level of willingness" along with "creating a lively workplace." The second is enhancement of each individual's abilities, and the third is the results of improvement which is undertaken by everyone in the circle. When these three aims are combined, QC can contribute to the development of the company.

Looking at it from the opposite direction, we may consider what steps we can take to create a lively workplace. There are a number of options, and QC circle activities is but one of them. These other options include: better and more fulfilling human relations between the superior and his subordinates, greater emphasis on recreation activities with each workplace as a unit and revitalization of the suggestion system.

In fact there is always a lively workplace, if a superior manages it in such a way that the willingness of each subordinate is raised and their collective individual abilities enhanced.

But the question comes down to this simple issue. "Can all managers and supervisors have that kind of concern? Do they manage well?" The answer, unfortunately, is often in the negative.

The QC circle has an advantage over other approaches. Its approaches are fairly well standardized and results are visible. This is why many companies prefer to utilize QC circles.

In utilizing QC circles, modifications may be necessary when applied in certain sectors. Lately we are extending QC circle activities to service divisions, marketing divisions, administrative divisions and technology-related divisions. JUSE's *General Principles of the QC Circle* was initially written for line workers. These principles can remain valid for service divisions and office workers, provided we know how to adapt them. For example, when we speak of voluntarism, we normally exclude those who are in managerial positions from active participation in circle activities. For the service sector, if managerial functions somehow make their way into QC circle activities, do not reject them. They may actually be of help in making QC circle activities become livelier. In such an instance, we can consider that the principle of voluntarism has been successfully adapted.

Question 3. Can QC Circle Help Bring Out Versatility?

When people happily engage in QC circle activities, can these lead to versatility? Can we consider this to be one of QC circle's objectives?

Answer

One of the objectives of the QC circle is to enhance each individual's abilities. As one participates in discussion, he may learn how to handle certain work which he is not doing presently. This can lead to versatility. However, unless he has a positive attitude, really wanting to participate in the work which he has never experienced or which is not his responsibility, he cannot learn. Then, of course, there is no opportunity for versatility. QC leaders must consider this issue when they meet with their groups.

Question 4. What Criteria Do You Use to Judge if a QC Circle Is Doing Well?

You have indicated many times that QC circle activities have been very lively at Toyoda Gosei. That's fine. But how can we judge how lively they are? Do you have evaluative standards or control items?

Answer

Yes, there are many evaluative standards, but the yardsticks we are using are as follows:

1. Self-evaluation for liveliness.

"Is your circle lively?" is the question asked of all the leaders and they must choose one of the following answers: "Yes, definitely," "Somewhat" or "No, it is not."

Of course, answers can be subjective, being a self-evaluation. We do not deny that unevenness remains for this evaluative criterion.

2. Number of meetings held.

Our guideline states that QC circles must meet twice a month, with each meeting lasting about an hour or so. But there are some circles which meet for 15 minutes during the noon break, and this is also counted as one meeting. Thus, in many workplaces, an average of three meetings a month is not uncommon.

As an auxiliary yardstick, it may be desirable to have the total number of hours met. But if you establish too many different yardsticks, you are bound to hear a complaint, saying: "Everytime we hold a QC circle meeting, we have to make a cumbersome report." Don't forget that QC circle activities are voluntary in nature. Never create a situation where the members abandon the activities, because of their dislike for making a report.

3. Rate of attendance.
4. Rate of participation in discussion.

I place a special emphasis on this. If a participant comes to a meeting which lasts for an hour and leaves it without saying a word, he may not feel that he has really participated. Make sure that everyone speaks up.

5. Number of suggestions received.
6. Number of themes solved.
7. Number of times participating in presentation meetings.
8. Atmosphere of the meeting, general conditions.

Here we ask for an intuitive evaluation by the leader. He does not have to make a report each time the circle holds a meeting, but he is asked to respond to a questionnaire once or twice a year. The questionnaire includes the following questions:

a. Do you maintain a jolly atmosphere? Noisy perhaps?
b. Do you think participants are happy to join in the circle activities?
c. Do members speak to each other freely outside QC meetings?
d. Do members actively support each other? Is your atmosphere conducive to good cooperation?
9. How well is the QC circle managed?
10. How well do the foreman and other interested parties support the circle's activities?

The secretariat makes a graph to get an overview of these items to make its evaluation.

The most important thing to remember is that by making QC circle activities lively, workers' attitude toward work changes.

I use an expression, "Their eyes shine differently." Please don't ask me how I can measure the shine of another person's eyes. But it's there. Someday, I hope a measuring device can be invented for us!

Question 5. Can a QC Circle Omit a Theme Relating to Maintenance Control?

Mr. Nemoto, you say that the themes to be selected by QC circles must be those related to improvement activities. As for themes relating to maintenance control, they are not to be taken up for discussion. But doesn't this go counter to what the General Principles of the QC Circle says? It mentions that themes on "control and improvement" must be taken up for discussion. Please explain further.

Answer

I have dealt with this issue earlier, but first we must make one thing clear; that is, the proper job function of a worker in the front line is to do the work in accordance with the work standards set for him. If he finds an abnormality, he must report it immediately to his supervisor. If he knows the cause or measures to be taken, he must give his opinion then. In this case, the work in question may be handled by one worker, or may be done by two workers.

Everything which is described above does not pertain to QC circle activities. Of course, when five or 10 workers are joined in a QC circle to discuss these issues, the same worker(s) may be present. These are the same people who perform their proper job functions. But what they do for their job functions and what they discuss at the QC circles are two separate things.

Next, I must restate my position that emphasis must not be placed exclusively on the results of improvement in establishing objectives for QC circles. Seeking results of improvement is the proper function of supervisors. They can ask the workers for their opinions and for their help in investigating and analyzing, but they do so by commanding, and that again comes from their proper job function.

The automobile industry is a labor intensive industry. Many line workers engage in repetitive manufacturing day after day. Maintenance control becomes part of their proper job function. The task of improvement is left for their superiors or the supervisors.

QC circles are introduced to raise the workers' consciousness toward quality and heighten their morale. It is our hope that when they look at their own work they will want to make improvements on it, and always ask and try to respond to this question: "Isn't there a better way of doing this?" The individual suggestion system has a similar purpose behind it.

Therefore at our QC circle activities, we prefer to see how well we get along and make our meeting a jolly one, overriding other considerations. Creating a lively workplace takes precedence over "how much money the company has made."

At many QC circle conferences, some foremen prefer to report about projects for which only one subordinate was asked to help, but treat them as QC circle activities. This is a serious mistake. These projects must be reported to the conference for foremen and not to the QC conference. Some equipment-handling companies lump together foremen's improvement activities with QC circle activities. Again this is wrong, and the company must redefine their respective roles.

Some people may say, "Line workers do engage in maintenance activities; therefore, it is appropriate for them to have themes dealing with maintenance. . . ."

But this is the way I think. It is true that line workers engage in maintenance work before they have to follow the standards set for them. However, when maintenance activities are translated into themes for QC circle activities, they take the following forms: "Let us abide by the standards," and "Let us report promptly when an abnormality occurs." I cannot think of any themes less interesting than these. They hear these admonitions all the time from their foreman. It is not fair to impose these same themes on them at QC circle meetings. No wonder so few people will be interested in attending.

Some other people will then add: "After improvements are made the process is standardized. Don't you call standardized work 'maintenance'?" Here the term standardization is used. It is a term which is found in the QC story for improvement. If a certain work is improved, the following must happen: standardization, no backsliding and prevention of recurrence. When an improvement theme is adopted, it will always lead to standardization. If QC circle members see this process and can understand that "work standards are established by the accumulation of technology in this fashion," they become more apt to follow standards in their daily work. We do not have to duplicate their efforts by selecting the theme of maintenance control for our QC circles.

Question 6. Do You Need a Companywide Guideline to Establish the Hours When Circles Can Meet?

In your previous talk, you mentioned that there is a need for establishing a guideline for the hours that the circles can meet. Is there a need for a companywide guideline?

Answer

At Toyoda Gosei, line workers in the workplace constitute the main body of all QC circle participants, and our policy for them is as follows: "Each month, you may meet for two hours or so outside your regular hour of work, and we shall pay your overtime for these hours." However, there are some groups in the workplace who can meet during regular working hours. They are people in preventive maintenance and die exchange. In such cases, if they want to meet during the regular hours, it is perfectly fine with us.

As for technology-related divisions, reduction of defectives and an increase in yield are part of their regular work, so they cannot be treated the same as other QC circles.

Most of the topics which are taken up as themes by QC circles are part of the regular responsibilities of the technology-related divisions. However, themes like a 10 percent increase in efficiency are good themes which can be discussed by other people after the regular hours of work. In technology-related areas, presentation meetings can be in a small-group setting. If only about 10 people from one section engage in a discussion of a 10 percent increase in efficiency or other themes, we encourage it. At Toyoda Gosei we give it the name of "group activities."

Even in technology-related divisions, there is some repetitious work done by female workers. Their activities are called QC circles. This kind of differentiation equally applies to marketing, purchasing and accounting divisions.

Question 7. Do You Need to Have Meetings in the Technology-Related Divisions Which Are Separate from Managerial Functions?

In your response to Question 6, you spoke of group activities at your technology-related divisions. Do they include those people who have managerial responsibilities? Do the meetings become similar to study sessions? In special cases like this, do you still think it is necessary to separate their meetings from the meetings of people in managerial positions?

Answer

The issue is not so much how meetings are organized as how superiors may obtain opinions from their subordinates. It is also important for subordinates to feel comfortable in voicing their opinions in a constructive and positive manner.

If the superior knows how to handle it, we do not have to give the name of group activities to a meeting. It can just as well be a study session, and there can still be ample opportunities for everyone to speak up. A meeting to discuss a 10 percent increase in efficiency, or another to raise the level of proper techniques, may be held by people in managerial positions on their own initiative. Actually it may be more appropriate if they do.

But at Toyoda Gosei we still have these group activities. It will take time before we can switch to meetings held by those in managerial positions.

Question 8. Can QC Circles Implement Improvement Goals?

I am, of course, in favor of QC circles taking up the problems of improvement. But when facilities have to be changed drastically, do you think QC circles should be involved?

Answer

Indeed these QC circles tackle the problems of improvement, but their proper involvement ends with making an improvement plan. Thereafter they may submit their plan to those who are in managerial positions. After they receive the plan, the management may study the budget required, examine the relation of the proposed plan to the company's other future plans and determine if the submitted plan is feasible. If a large-scale renovation is required for facilities, it may take several months to implement. Thus it is not advisable for QC circles to take up this type of problem too early in the game. In a large project, a QC circle will do well to ask that those problems of improvement relating to work standards be taken up first by management, and then ask the management to confirm the results.

When I go to a presentation meeting, many QC circles will claim that they have done everything. They know that some of the projects cannot be implemented without management's active assistance. They must candidly mention that fact in their reports.

Question 9. What to Look for When a Superior Wants to Give Suggestions for Alternative Themes?

Mr. Nemoto, you say that during the initial period, superiors must provide several alternative themes for QC circles to choose from. How can we perform this task effectively? Please give us some pointers.

Answer

The most important consideration in selecting a theme is to be sure that everyone can discuss that theme with a measure of enthusiasm.

Generally, if no results can ensue after an improvement plan is initiated, willingness to take up the next theme may dissipate. On the other hand, if too much emphasis is placed on the results, the theme itself may become a difficult one to solve. That will hinder the creation of a congenial atmosphere.

Improvement activities undertaken by those in managerial positions normally start with those themes which can bring out significant results. But QC circles must also remain faithful to the position of placing priority on "everyone speaks," and themes must be chosen accordingly.

Question 10. How Do You Handle the Issue of Training Members of QC Circles?

Presently we can deal with the training of QC circle leaders, but we have not been able to extend that training to all the members. I understand that at Toyoda Gosei you have been able to provide education for all participants. How did you do it?

Answer

May I supply an example from our Haruhi plant?

In the spring of 1984, QC circle members at the Haruhi plant requested that we not confine our QC education to the leaders but extend it to them. They wanted to learn the techniques of QC, and especially the seven tools. The plant immediately established its own program.

Normally when this kind of request is received, the TQC promotion office will be asked to draft a plan with the quality assurance division providing instructors. The Haruhi plant did not follow this procedure. It decided to formulate a plan entirely on its own. They divided their 500 members into five groups and decided to use five Saturdays for their study sessions. As for instructors, there were 10 section chiefs in the plant (including those chiefs who were with line workers). Of these, two each would serve as instructors for a respective session.

The 10 section chiefs decided to prepare their own QC text based on actual examples from the Haruhi plant, a move which insured that everyone could understand the subject. The actual instructional meetings were held on Saturdays, and there was no overtime paid for attendance. But the rate of attendance was close to 100 percent. The post-session questionnaire confirmed what we already knew. These instructional sessions were very popular.

In most other instances, it is true that after we finish QC education for QC circle leaders, we hardly have time to extend that education to all the members. But the Haruhi plant has somehow managed to provide an outstanding education.

One more thing which I wish to emphasize in Haruhi's education plan is that all 10 section chiefs, including those who supervise line workers, participated in the project as instructors. To teach about QC circle's objectives and the techniques of using seven tools of QC required a lot of preparation. I know an enormous amount of effort has gone into it.

221

The enthusiasm that these section chiefs exhibited naturally was transmitted to QC circle members. This, in turn, contributed significantly to the vitality that all of us experienced in their QC circle activities.

Question 11. What Does Mr. Nemoto Have in Mind When He Says He Wants a "Lively Workplace"?

At a speech before the Japan Society of Quality Control held in Nagoya, you used a new table to explain your concept of a lively workplace. Can you share that table with us?

Answer

In that speech, I emphasized the following points.

What do I expect of QC circle activities? I do not want them to be lively just at the time QC circle meetings are held. I want them to be lively when they are engaged in their proper functions.

This new table (Table 11–2) deals with work conditions in the workplace. Thus it has columns only for maintenance control and improvement. (If technology-related items are to be included, development must be placed under a separate column.)

For each of the functions performed, step-by-step, the table separates that which is to be performed by the supervisor (and the staff if called for) and by common line workers. Signs ◎ and ○ are placed there. Column A indicates how proper functions are determined in companies and they are represented by sign ◎ . The other sign ○ indicates the areas of QC circle activities. Also by engaging in QC circle activities, it is expected that even those classified as proper functions may also become lively, as indicated in Column B with ⁙ .

For example, by observing standards, the ◎ sign in Column A becomes a boldfaced sign ◉ in Column B. That indicates that the manner of observance of the standards is expected to be much stricter than before. There are arrow signs pointing both ways between a small ○ sign and a big double ◉ sign for supervisors. These arrow signs indicate that supervisors may from time to time call on line workers and say to them "Come and help me out on this," or "I want to have your opinion on this." By asking line workers to participate in the work of a supervisor, it is expected that their ability may be enhanced and their consciousness about quality raised. All of these functions can lead to the creation of a livelier and happier workplace.

It is not interesting to the workers to abide by standards which were forced upon them before. No good work can come out of it.

	Step	(A) Proper function		(B) Expected result	
		Supervisor (and staff)	Line workers	Supervisor (and staff)	Line workers
Maintenance—control	1. Determining standards	◎		◎←──→○	
	2. Observance of standards		◎		◎
	3. Checking off standard items	◎		◎←──○	
	4. Discovery of abnormalities and reporting	○	◎		◎
	5. Countermeasures and prevention of recurrence	◎		◎←──→○	
Difficult improvement	1. Investigation and analysis	◎		◎←──→○	
	2. Studying improvement plans	◎		◎←──→○	
	3. Trial run and implementation	◎		◎←──→○	
	4. Evaluation and standardization	◎		◎←──→○	
Not difficult improvement	1. Investigation and analysis	◎	⊙(dotted)	◎←──→○	⊙(dotted)
	2. Studying improvement plans	◎	○(dotted)	◎←──→○	⊙(dotted)
	3. Trial run and implementation	◎		◎←──→○	
	4. Evaluation and standardization	◎	○(dotted)	◎←──→○	⊙(dotted)

(Left margin spanning labels: "Maintenance—control" and "Improvement")

Table 11-2: Creation of a Lively Workplace

Question 12. Is the Creation of a Lively Workplace also Necessary for the Staff Divisions?

Mr. Nemoto, you mentioned that at Toyoda Gosei, QC circle activities center around the workplace, and staff members are treated differently. For the latter, QC activities are still on a trial basis. I think the staff members must also create a lively workplace for themselves. In the process of your experimentation with this and other divisions, have you found some new approaches which you can share with us?

Answer

We are still at the stage of experimentation, so we cannot provide any firm conclusion. However, may I call your attention to Category B in the Table on small group activities (Table 11–1). Please give some thought to how it may be managed. A staff division may consist of only a few members under a division manager or a section chief. If they have to pick themes, they may select themes like "improvement in the degree of precision" or "shortening the daily routine" which are concerned directly with improvement activities. Naturally these themes reflect very strongly the desire of their superior who holds a managerial position. In some instances, some subsection chiefs may be asked to serve as leaders in the meetings to which the section chief may also be present. One basic criterion for the success of these meetings is the ability of people to speak up freely. A lively workplace requires that the place be endowed with an atmosphere in which everyone can speak.

If the superior can create such an atmosphere, there will be no need to have additional group activities or special meetings. The regular meetings they have as part of their work will suffice. However, unfortunately not too many managers have this ability. So at least for now, we must hold separate meetings under the name of "group activities," to create a congenial atmosphere.

As a theme for these meetings, my suggestion is "efficiency in office work."

Question 13. How to Give Superiors the Leadership Ability Required for QC Circles?

In the case of Toyota Motors, success for QC circle activities was assured because you started from the top and gradually went down the ranks finally reaching the line workers. In our company, the top and line workers started QC at the same time. We lack leadership ability. How can we handle this problem?

Answer

Many companies which have begun QC in recent years have generally let both the top and line workers start QC at the same time. Under this kind of condition, it is important for the top to be one step ahead of the rest. They can, for example, increase the frequency of study for this purpose. If the top acquires enough skills to be able to evaluate QC circle presentations, things can move rather smoothly. On this issue, please refer to Chapter 5 of Part I.

Question 14. In Speaking of Assistance Which Superiors Can Provide, You Have Not Included Positive Evaluation of QC. Is There a Reason for Its Omission?

In Chapter 6 of Part I, you spoke of making a report in three minutes. In my opinion, the reason for the success of these three-minute presentations lies in the ability of the superior to provide positive reinforcement. To discover an abnormality and report it, and to discover something which is off standard and correct it, are routine activities. But praise from a superior follows the report to make it into something very special.

Given this success, then, why don't you include an item in your list of "steps a superior in the workplace can take to help QC circles" as follows: "A superior must evaluate in a positive manner the results of QC circle activities or activities themselves."

Answer

I fully agree with you. If a superior evaluates and praises his subordinate's work, the latter will indeed be more positively inclined to do good work.

Let me give a couple of examples. You can go to a QC circle meeting for just a couple of minutes, but you can still say: "Good, keep up the good work." You can perhaps choose another occasion to tell its leader that you were impressed "to see the manner in which everyone spoke up, and the way in which they engaged in the analysis of cause factors." These little things can provide positive reinforcement.

Question 15. Can You Provide Some Examples of Small Group Activities in Administrative Divisions?

Table 11–1's categorization of small group activities is a very interesting one. If you have some examples of matters relating to B, please explain them to us.

Answer

At Toyoda Gosei, QC circle activities center around the workplace, and there are no unified activities on a companywide basis for small group activities held by administrative or technology-related divisions. In some job categories, it may be better to have activities which are

225

combined with the meetings of those who are in management positions. We are experimenting with various approaches.

Let me give you an example from our computer division. This workplace consists of a highly skilled professional group, and their activities cannot be treated in the same way QC circle activities are treated in other workplaces. However, we felt that they could still get together on a theme of "efficiency in our work," and so an improvement project was initiated.

The group decided to narrow down the theme to "efficiency in developing and writing programs." Through their group activities, a standardized project was completed. It was called "creating patterns for our various computer programs."

This division, incidentally, creates many computer programs in cooperation with other divisions and offices, and their involvement is companywide. As a result, many of their activities fall under Category G in Table 11–1. A good example of the result of this cooperation is the development of START, or the system of controlling daily routine for production preparation. Incidentally, this project took two years to complete (see p. 141).

Question 16. At Divisional Presentation Meetings, Do You Give Improvement Examples from Groups or Individuals?

I understand that you hold separate presentation meetings by division for your office management and administrative divisions. Do the examples presented always result from group activities? Do you have examples of activities by individuals?

Answer

The answer is both. The example in Question 15 from the computer division is a group project.

However, in our office management and administrative divisions, there are some types of work which are handled by single individuals. Improvement for that type of work is often conceptualized by one individual and carried out by him alone. Of course, before he implements his improvement plan, he must secure his superior's approval. But in confirming the results of improvement and effecting standardization, no one else is involved. When he translates his work into a QC story, it becomes his story to tell to the rest.

Themes like this need not be converted into group activities. At the presentation meeting, the presenter can say: "I have made these improvements. May I have your attention concerning what I say, and I should appreciate your candid opinions to help me improve further."

At our accounting division, in order to promote improvement and to enhance everyone's ability, monthly improvement presentation meetings are held. All 40 members of this division attend these meetings. On the topic of enhancing employee ability, each individual is required to give two reports a year. The report may be presented by one person, by two people or by a larger group. Section chiefs take turns commenting by theme, and at the end of each meeting the division manager gives his overall evaluation.

Question 17. What Is the Secret of Your Rehearsal?

You speak of the importance of utilizing rehearsal as a means of instructing QC members. I understand that you made so many rehearsals at home some 20 years ago when Toyota Motors was audited for the Deming prize that Mrs. Nemoto also became an expert on QC. In fact, she can make her own QC presentation. Is this really true?

Answer

The story has been exaggerated somewhat, especially when you say that my wife can make her own presentation. I was a division manager at Toyota Motors in 1965 when the company received the Deming prize. There were many occasions on which I had to make my presentation, and I stayed home late at night to engage in my rehearsal.

As I did this every night, my wife became familiar with a number of QC techniques. One day she told me: "Please listen to me. I did my own quality control." Her story follows:

"When spring comes, one-half of my wash gets decorated with bird droppings, and I have to wash it all over again. I wanted to know why droppings occurred in this fashion. After I hung all my wash, I observed carefully. And then it became clear to me. These birds come to our yard to eat box tree seeds. After they are fed, they fly to our next door neighbor. While they fly droppings reach my wash. But it was not clear to me why only one-half of my wash was affected. There were three bamboo poles available for use that day. Among the three, the wash placed on the third pole had the worst incidences of droppings. So I used your stratification method to judge the wash on these three poles.

"Now everything was clear. The wash on the first pole, which was nearest our eaves, contained not a single dropping, but the second pole had half-clean and half-soiled wash. The third one had wash completely covered with droppings. The conclusion was obvious. The droppings were accumulated while the birds flew over the third pole. My observation confirmed it.

"Now the question was why the birds prefer to fly over the third pole. My conclusion was that they did not want to fly too near the eaves which would be dangerous to them. Birds want to fly unhindered in a wide-open space.

"I decided to take action by creating obstacles for these birds. I set up several bamboo poles with one side of the pole on the ground and the other side protruding in the air. Next day, as expected, the birds flew through the outer circle to avoid my bamboo poles. There was not a single trace of droppings on my wash. I had zero defects!"

My wife's story ends there.

You must have heard this story in an exaggerated form. What I wanted to say when I first made this story public was that I rehearsed and rehearsed so many times in those days.

INDEX

231

INDEX